Desert Song

God's Eternal Song of Love

J Morris Smith

authorHOUSE®

AuthorHouse™
1663 Liberty Drive
Bloomington, IN 47403
www.authorhouse.com
Phone: 1-800-839-8640

First published by AuthorHouse 7/30/2009

ISBN: 978-1-4490-0739-3 (sc)

Cover by Wendy Clark, grand-daughter of the author.
www.wendyclarkdesign@gmail.com

Printed in the United States of America
Bloomington, Indiana

This book is printed on acid-free paper.

DEDICATION

To Barby, with whom I have been so blessed
to sing and dance to Love's Song for fifty years,
transforming the discords of pride and conceit
into choreography characteristic of Christ's love
for His bride, the church.

DESERT SONG
God's eternal song of love

PROLOGUE

     The desert possesses a rhythm - a rhythm that only the eremitic climate can produce, that effects the landscape and the skyscape, the daybreak and the sunset, the whispers of the night and the illusions of the day. It's one of Creation's most beautiful productions.

     Throughout sacred history, the desert has been used by God to mature, strengthen, reconcile, redeem, convict, and call the people of the great plan of salvation. Abraham, Moses, David, Elijah, John the Baptist, Paul, John, and even Jesus were led or sent to the desert before and often during their part in the outworking of God's great purpose for all made in His image and likeness. Such sojourns form the stanzas of His great song of love.

God's Love sings a desert song,
     that creates from the dry.
With Their Word They fill the void,
     from nothing They ordain.
The Song begins before the first…
     continues past the end.
Its lyrics are both pure and true,
     eternal's holy blend.

The deserts of our journey come
     from deep within ourselves…
The sands are of our own design…
     the fear of Love itself.
But there God calls us each to hear
     Love's echo and embrace.
Eternal Love is found in Them,
     and shared with His own race.

When found surrounded by our pride,
      the chaos of the dry…
Listen…Listen…to the Voice
      requiring faith renewed.
In garden spoiled or bush aflame
      or wilderness of sin
The desert song will call in love,
      for Love is heard therein.

God's Love sings a desert song,
      appealing to the soul…
This Song the spirit doth inflame,
      and sets the conscience free.
For time cannot bind the Love,
      nor space create a range,
And history is vapor made,
      but Love's Song is unchanged.

METHOD

Written in common meter,
   four line stanza (quatrain),
   the syllable order being 8,6,8,6,
   with rhyme of ABCC.

Each Canto covers a particular section of Sacred History.

Each quatrain is numbered for
referencing the Scriptures found in the
Appendix..

Certain sacred stories, prophecies, and
imageries are telescoped to emphasize
the principle without losing the overall
theme of the canto.

A singing term may be used to replace
a speaking word without losing any
meaning.

GLOSSARY

Canto - any of the main divisions of certain long poems, like chapters in a book.

Love - when capitalized refers to the Father, first person of the Trinity.

One - when capitalized refers to the Son, second person of the Trinity.

Wind, Breath - when capitalized, refers to the Holy Spirit, third Person of the Trinity.

Voice - when capitalized, designates the Word, Second Person of the Trinity.

Song - when capitalized, designates the redemption message of God.

Their, Them, They, etc. - when capitalized, refers to the Holy Trinity.

LORD - all letters capitalized, refers to the "I AM".

Seer - the Hebrew word *nabi*, translated "prophet".

LOVE'S SONG

CANTO OF LOVE'S SONG

When all was not and time was not,
       but formless, dark, and nil,
The barrenness was not as thought
       where chaos seemed to rule.
The One who sings was in its space,
       A triune harmony,
A realm was there where Love did reign
       in timeless Mystery. (1)

Though unperceived, the void is full
       of Love forever True.
Timeless, perfect, no past to fear
       nor future to inscribe.
Pervading all and knowing all
       and potent through and through,
The origin of Truth and Right,
       the fount of all that's due. (2)

The Song of Love reveals a Heart
     in ways hereto unheard,
And shapeless void becomes the clef
     for notes of Love Divine.
Hovering there on surface deep,
     is Holy Wind of Might,
To take what comes from spoken Word
     and order it aright. (3)

A spoken word is not defined
     by meaning all alone,
But by inflection of the voice,
     the breath, the spirit's choice.
So Love has motive and design,
     and Voice brings what's believed,
And Wind's arrangement orders right,
     perfection's goal achieved. (4)

Eon-ic days of timeless time,
     how else can it be known?
For Love is unaccountable
     to laws of time and space.
It is the Who and not the how
     in Whom the Song's composed,
And in the desert Word carves out
     what Sacred Love disposed. (5)

From spoken Word and shaping Breath,
      came first the light and sky,
Followed by terrestrial signs
      that made the angels gasp.
Then, set in range ethereal,
      the sun to rule the day
And moon to seasons regulate
      and stars to guide the way. (6)

All kinds of creatures, large and small,
      for sea and sky alike
Came next to occupy the land
      and teem in water's berth.
Then living stock to romp about,
      each after its own kind.
Along the ground they came in turn,
      to be as Love consigned. (7)

And all in heaven and on earth
      a truth and order found.
Each was unique in nature's scheme,
      yet webbed in symphony.
For each thing made depends on each,
      as fixed in life's demands
Ere strong or weak, each one submits
      to fit in Truth's commands. (8)

Then came the Word that startled all
        angelic myriads,
For what they heard gave reason for
        this universal work.
All that's been done has been so done
        to make a perfect place,
And what came next would cause a stir
        and stun celestial's race. (9)

All of creation came about
        for this one purpose true.
The mystery that Love reveals
        is sung with Triune Joy,
"Let Us make one like unto Us,
        and with Our Image grace,
That he may share the Love We have
        in this terrestrial place. (10)

"Above all else We'll let him rule,
        in ocean, sky, and land,
And every plant and tree he'll have
        to meet his heart's desire.
We'll put in him Our awesome Love
        and care for every need,
Protect him and rejoice in him,
        for this is good indeed. (11)

"In Our image he, too, will love,
  Our Love he will embrace,
We'll share Our glorious reign with him
  and all he'll procreate.
Unlike the angels We command
  and even those We lost,
Knowing Our Love he will respond
  in love with love's great cost. (12)

"Yet, We'll make sure that he'll be free
  to choose the loving Way,
For what would be the joy to Us
  if loved without a voice.
Our joy will always be in him
  and for him We will care:
Our Song of Love is his to sing,
  his heart with Ours to share." (13)

They did not make man with the Word,
  but from created stuff,
Of unshaped dust and water fresh
  They molded with the mud.
And with Their Breath this mortal-ness
  They reverently imbued.
With heart and soul and spirit grant,
  divine similitude. (14)

In Their image They made the man,
      and Holy likeness gave,
Then from the male, a female took,
      the second from the first.
Dividing up and closing then
      in anesthesia's sleep,
Becoming two, remaining one,
      for shameless love to keep. (15)

In a garden they were put
      to give it care and keep,
With every need provided there,
      and daily walk Divine.
So judgment of what's right and wrong
      is given in this place.
No need to strive with good and bad,
      but listen to the Grace. (16)

Thus, there they lived beatified
      for days and nights on end,
With death unknown, in timeless pause,
      no sense of life's decay,
But work the work of God's desire,
      Love's purpose to fulfill,
Contented with serenity
      to sing in Love Song's trill. (17)

How long this was does not compute,
    for there's no time herein,
But, bliss of Love for Them and they,
    eternal life to live.
Knowledge of the good and bad
    was constantly supplied,
Partaking of the words of God
    was their provision plied. (18)

CANTO OF LOVE REJECTED

The man and woman truly one,
  between them there's no space.
Their nakedness was openness,
  no secret to conceal.
No shame was theirs in paradise
  for guilt had not yet scored,
And interlocked as interlocked
  their spirits were adored. (1)

Before the Word had made the light
  or Wind had ordered space,
God's first in charge of angel band
  had challenged for Their place.
The morning star, the son of dawn,
  said in his heart's dismay,
"I will ascend, I will enthrone,
  I will become as They." (2)

The boast was grave, the challenge made,
       and certain angels bid:
Sin so conceived and sin lived out
       is always from within.
"I will…I will…I will…I will…"
       is first of love to thwart,
Resentment, then, will set in place
       and sure delusion start. (3)

So Lucifer, the prince of lights,
       became the prince of dark,
And those who made the bid with him
       were cast beyond the Realm
To roam the chaos of the deep,
       the abyss of what's out,
Where no sound's found of Love's sweet Song,
       but anger, wrath, and doubt. (4)

When Word made light and Wind moved forth
       to order it aright,
This wicked one was stirred from death
       with curiosity.
He came to new creation's range
       to see Love Song's effect,
And there disguised as serpent wise
       till hate's plan he'd perfect. (5)

Then snakes were thought to know it all,
      'specially ways of life,
So prey to Satan's trickery
      the mighty serpent fell.
And from that stage the devil sang
      to spoil Love's sacred theme;
For if he can't be one with Them,
      then neither should these deem. (6)

"Did God so say..." will cause the doubt;
      "You cannot..." be the dodge.
To set the trap and lead the way
      would be his subtle game.
He only knows one willful way
      to cause this mortal's bane...
'Tis all he did and all he can,
      self-will is still the same. (7)

For this-a-way the love is blocked
      and will not go each way,
Resentment seeps into the heart,
      imagination plays.
The doubt occasions questions first,
      then next confusion reigns,
And love has lost its full impact
      to honor and abstain. (8)

"Has God so said you can't partake
        of any tree that's here?"
"Oh, yes, we can…but not that tree,
        the one that's in the midst.
Ev'n if we touch it we will die,
        the Lord our God implied."
"Well, if you eat you will not die"
        the fallen angel lied. (9)

"But, They know that if you do eat
        you'll be as They, you see,
And then you'll know to live your life
        by your own judgment free.
With knowledge of the good and bad
        of all your own desire,
You'll always make the proper choice
        to do as you aspire." (10)

And so she looked, this woman pure,
        and saw the fruit was good,
A blessing to the eye, as well,
        and one thing more she thought:
To keep her from her own will is
        not fair of Trinity,
To learn to live by her own choice,
        so right and just she'll be. (11)

And thrice deceived she reached and took
        what looked to her the best.
She ate the fruit that Love forbade,
        and truth was then denied.
The man was there at her arm's reach,
        but did not use the grace
To step up to the evil one,
        secure in Love's embrace. (12)

Then as she reached to give to him
        the willful act of self,
He took the fruit and ate it down
        as his own coward's due.
Pride thus entered pure paradise
        disrupting Love's Song's ode,
And altered Love's most precious gain,
        where image was bestowed. (13)

It's Adam's sin 'tis said till now,
        for he stood not his ground,
And by that fault all born to him
        the stain of sin will bear.
That he henceforth will so retain
        the label and the blame
For her rash act in his purview
        will be put with his name. (14)

So then they looked with guilt and shame
        to see most painfully
Their own perverseness of the act
        that creates life anew.
Unbearable it was for them
        to face each other's fault,
So stinging leaves of figs were fit
        for punishment they sought. (15)

CANTO OF LOVE'S FIDELITY

In disrepute they could not look
     on each the other's sin,
They hid from Them among the trees
     to shelter their disgrace.
When Love came walking in the Wind
     to sing the morning song,
They fled in fear before the Voice
     because they had done wrong. (1)

But Love will not be put off long,
     for love is far too strong,
And lifting Voice to make the plaint
     as He will often do,
For now the One who is the Word
     of Love's creation song
Will be the One to give the call
     as Love's salvation's balm. (2)

But, there that day the Voice had walked
     amid creation's pain.
He called in love to those He lost,
     so they'd respond in need.
Intoned in Voice of grave concern,
     "Where are you?" was Love's claim,
"I'm hiding in my nakedness,"
     the timid answer came. (3)

How would the man know "nakedness,"
     the good and bad of that?
And Voice knew well from whence there came
     that judgment to be known.
"The tree…you've taken from the tree
     that We said not to eat."
Wanting conviction in the heart,
     the waiting was discrete. (4)

"I did so eat," the man confessed,
     "but it was she who served!"
"I did indeed," she did concede,
     "by snake I was deceived."
Avowal made, they stood in pain
     of knowing what they ate.
In fallen state new feelings came
     to stay and saturate. (5)

So to the foil, that snake possessed,
      the Holy Voice rang out:
"Cursed are you above all the rest,
      you will eat dust for life.
A wedge We'll put between your seed
      and that of hers as well.
You'll strike His heel, He'll crush your head
      and save the one who fell." (6)

Though Love abused is still pure love,
      the suffering is real;
Love makes the promise to restore,
      and make the healing sure.
Though desert will result from this
      and paradise be banned,
In eremitic notes Love's Song
      will sing in wind and sand. (7)

"You are mother of all life,"
      the Voice was heard to say,
Through pain she'll birth, submit to man,
      is what her penance is.
"The ground is cursed because of you"
      the Voice intoned to man,
Thorns will vex his work on earth,
      by sweat his life will span. (8)

Man's rest will come when his life's done,
    and in the ground he'll lay.
From dust he's made with love and care,
    and given life from Life.
To dust he shall again return
    to wait his destiny,
For Love's too strong a cord to break,
    he'll live eternally. (9)

Love then gave them garments of skin,
    the blood first shed for sin,
"They have become like us," God said,
    knowing the good, the bad.
Love drove them from the tree of life,
    lest they're forever led,
For Love cannot abide the thought
    of always living dead. (10)

Now time will bend and space will yield
    and history defend,
And sin will be the common thing,
    for all will fall to pride.
But, this globe's built on righteousness,
    and truth is at its core.
When violence and untruth spread,
    Love will such pride abhor. (11)

So Love's compelled to sing the Song,
      to sing the desert song
Of cleansing of the earth and sky,
      with water from above.
To baptize all that pride had duped,
      leave nothing unredeemed.
What's wicked had become the way,
      to render self-esteem. (12)

But, Love's Song is a desert song,
      and in those distant days
When pride perverted Love's intent,
      and all was in decay,
When Love grieved over what They saw,
      yet, righteousness remained,
For righteous Noah walked with Love,
      and sang Truth's sacred strains. (13)

Love's Song was then sung as a dirge,
      to Noah and his clan,
Of flood to come to cleanse the earth,
      and loose creation's pain.
"Build an ark," Love' Song sang out,
      a boat to glean the Life.
Water will be salvation's tide
      restoring free of strife. (14)

A new beginning came about
     with covenant and oath:
Love will not curse the ground again
     for mankind's sinful ways,
But, sing a song of love's strong tie
     for persons yet unborn,
The rainbow for a sign was giv'n,
     to mark the renewed morn. (15)

THE DESERT SONG

THE CANTO OF ABRAHAM

The Song calls Abram far away
  from all he's ever known,
From kith and kin, familiar place,
  to go to stranger's land.
He left it all to heed Love's call,
  Their blessing to embrace.
But he took Lot, his link to life,
  to wander desert space. (1)

"I'll bless your name and make it great,
  a nation you'll become.
Those who bless you, I too will bless,
  who curse you, I will curse.
And then through you I will fulfill
  the promise from above,
To bless all those throughout the earth
  with sacrifice of Love." (2)

So Abram left, the song foretold,
　　　and prospered in strange lands,
A desert wanderer became,
　　　well-known throughout the realm.
To spread his flocks and feed his herds,
　　　young Lot demanded space,
And took the plain well-watered there,
　　　with Sodom as the base. (3)

Now Lot is gone and Abram's back,
　　　now in the place first called,
To leave his father's house and all,
　　　and traverse by the Song.
And in this place so lately reached,
　　　the Song is sung again,
"I'll make your offspring like the sand
　　　and give you this for land." (4)

But, though Lot's gone, now Sarai's old
　　　and there's no child for them,
No heir for Abram far too old,
　　　the promise seemed to wane.
"As stars are countless in the sky,
　　　I'll make your offspring thrive."
The Sovereign Lord proclaimed it still,
　　　but how could it survive? (5)

So Abram's wife who bore no heir,
     had heard Love's desert song,
To ensure Love's song would prove true,
     she'd lend a helping hand.
She sent her maid as surrogate
     to birth a son for him,
And it seemed right to Abram's pride,
     for Love Song's vow grew dim. (6)

Then God appeared to Abram old,
     confirmed Their oath with him,
"Your numbers will be countless yet,
     and your possessions vast.
'Exalted father' Abram defined,
     no longer is your name,
'Father of many...Abraham,'
     will be your call to fame. (7)

And Sarai will be 'Sarah' now,
     for mother she will be,
For nations will come from her womb,
     and kings she'll surely bear.
A son you'll have from your own love,
     my promise made in troth,"
Love's Desert Song was sung that day
     to ratify the oath. (8)

The child of age was born to them
      just as was promise made.
The child of pride was sent away
      to face the desert's wrath.
But Love as sung to Abraham
      cannot revoke what's pledged,
The child of pride became renown,
      as Love's Song had alleged. (9)

Voice sings the Desert Song in love
      and righteousness and truth.
How odd it seemed to hear a Song
      of human sacrifice.
Why would He who gave the son
      require him at such cost?
Yet, Love indeed pronounced the need
      for such a holocaust. (10)

"Take this your son, your only son,
      the son of aged faith,
Provisions take and three days go,
      and offer him to Me."
Against Love's ways, it made no sense,
      yet faith had learned what's feared,
And three days out, on desert route,
      Moriah's height appeared. (11)

"Stay with the beast," the servant's told,
     "and we will yonder go.
The boy and I will worship there,
     and then come back to you."
The boy knew not as Abraham
     of Love's proscribed command,
What had he done to anger Them,
     that such be Their demand? (12)

"The wood is here, the fire you brought,
     but one thing's missing now,
Where is the lamb for sacrifice?"
     the boy so boldly asks.
"God Himself will provide the Lamb,"
     faithful was the reply.
A sacred victim slain for sin
     the Song would not deny. (13)

When reached the spot, an altar made,
     the boy was tied and placed.
The strength of youth could sure prevail,
     against the aged one.
Into the hands of father's will,
     he made himself the price,
As if ordained, the humble youth
     became the sacrifice. (14)

The knife was raised by faithful hand,
 the father's heart would break.
Through tear-filled eyes he aimed the blade
 at only son's pure heart.
Crescendo rang out loud and clear
 as earth stood still for them,
"Abraham," the Love's Voice sang out,
 "Lay not your hand on him. (15)

"For now I know, I truly know
 that you will trust in Me."
And looking up into the Voice,
 the old man saw the gift.
Behind him caught in thicket's branch,
 so recently passed near,
A ram would be the substitute
 and make atonement clear. (16)

A ram twill be and not a lamb,
 for this will be a sign,
Of Love's Song's most sacred theme
 throughout the days to come.
The Song will go, as seer's know,
 when on Moriah's butte,
Love Themselves will provide the Lamb,
 redemption to impute. (17)

Thus Abraham, in desert lore,
  had sung in harmony;
The promise that was guarantee
  did not deter his faith.
By offering the promised son,
  he trusted Love Song's dare,
Became the father of the faith
  that resurrection shares. (18)

Love's Song oft sings of those who came
  and in the desert played
With Them whose purpose they accept,
  whose destiny achieve.
Of Jacob wrestling with the Voice
  and seeing face to face,
And twelve sons to Israel birthed,
  as Love's own chosen race. (19)

Of Joseph cast in desert well
  and sold as Egypt's slave,
Love sings of his receiving grace
  to save the famished land.
Love was with him in this dry place
  with Pharaoh's favored care.
His father with his tents came down
  and formed a people there. (20)

Four hundred years they grew in masse
      'til threatening they were.
Then a pharaoh who knew them not,
      suppressed with brutal hand.
So land of fertile plain became
      a desert of despair.
In bondage they became the slaves,
      oppressed in pride's cruel snare. (21)

THE CANTO OF MOSES

In this grim time of bitterness,
      the Pharaoh's fears increased.
All males he sought to kill at birth,
      to keep rebellion down.
So every male that's Hebrew born ,
      was thrown into the Nile.
But Hebrew midwives feared the Lord,
      refusing to defile. (1)

A child was born of Levi's tribe,
      and hidden from the king.
Then in a basket he was placed
      and floated in the reeds.
The Pharaoh's daughter happened by,
      to walk along the bank.
She heard his cry; she took him home
      to raise in her own rank. (2)

In this time of suffering sore,
      Love's Song had not expired,
Their melody's sweet tune had caught
      the royal daughter's ear.
In seeking nurse to feed the child,
      his mother she'd retain.
In Pharaoh's house the child was raised,
      but Hebrew he'd remain. (3)

This child named Moses grew and saw
      his people's dreadful plight,
How hard their labor had become,
      and valueless their life.
Egyptian boss he one day killed
      for raising brutal hand.
In darkness he concealed the act
      and covered it with sand. (4)

The next day Moses intervened
      in irate Hebrew's fight,
And heard the words that froze his heart,
      his act had been exposed.
When Pharaoh heard of Moses' deed,
      his life was on demand,
So Moses fled from Pharaoh's wrath
      into the desert land. (5)

He came upon some nomads there,
     who took him as their own.
Kind Jethro, priest of Midian,
     a man of noble note,
His daughter Moses took to wed,
     and sons were born to him.
He settled in to herd the sheep,
     a future drab and dim. (6)

An alien in a foreign land,
     it seems that Love forsook.
Displaced from people of his own,
     refused by Egypt's code,
He wandered with the desert tribe,
     exiled, disgraced, restrained.
A prince of Egypt he had been,
     now, vagabond ordained. (7)

Love's Sequence had not near been sung,
     nor theme abandoned yet,
For Love had heard poor Israel's groan,
     and listened to their grief.
But Love's Song is a desert song,
     to reach the ready heart,
And give the call to one who's lost
     all pride and self-retort. (8)

While tending Jethro's flock one day
    near Horeb's holy mount,
There was a sight uncommon there
    that Moses could not grasp.
A bush afire, yet unconsumed,
    a strange thing to behold.
So he approached it cautiously,
    lest he should be too bold. (9)

"Moses, Moses" the Bush called out,
    the Voice was heard again!
"Here I am," was the meek reply,
    with timidness and fear.
Moses shrouded his face from Voice,
    afraid of the profound,
"Remove your sandals from your feet,
    you stand on holy ground. (10)

"I've seen the mis'ry of my love,
    and hate their suffering.
I'm sending you to bring them out,
    the Love Song you will sing."
"How can I go and sing this Song?
    The people won't believe.
They'll think that I've become quite mad.
    They surely will not leave. (11)

"And Who shall I say sent me there?
        The God who has no name?
The God of old has sent me here?
        No, they'll not understand.
This people are so sore oppressed,
        suspicious they've become,
Without a name they pay no heed,
        no argument be won." (12)

"I AM WHO I AM", Voice proclaimed
        so very calm and clear,
"This is what must be sung to them,
        when asked Who sent you there.
I AM has sent because He cares,
        the God of Abraham,
The God of Isaac, Jacob, too,
        His Name is The I AM. (13)

"Then to the elders you shall sing,
        the promise made is true,
I AM has come to take you out
        of misery and death.
To take you to a place of rest,
        sworn to the fathers past,
A promised land of rich delight
        will be your home at last." (14)

But Moses argued with the Lord
        for fear of going back,
And asked for signs to prove his place,
        confirming desert call.
"What if they'll not believe in me,
        I have no proof to give
That You appeared to me at all,
        a transient fugitive?" (15)

His staff was thrown upon the ground,
        a serpent it became,
"The staff will be your proof of call;
        now pick it up again."
He thrust his hand within his cloak,
        it turned a leprous shade,
"Now put it back and see My work
        of restoration made." (16)

"I'm slow of speech, my tongue is halt,
        so please send someone else,
I am the least that you could use",
        poor Moses pleaded still.
"So use your brother, Aaron, then"
        the Voice in anger said.
For I AM puts forth all the Words;
        I AM have prophets led. (17)

"Now take this staff and use it well,
        their deliverer be,
Is it not I Who causes sight
        and all the senses grace?
I could not use you until now,
        a pharaoh's prince with fame,
But, now you've nothing left to boast,
        you're ready for Our claim. (18)

"Those are all dead who sought your life,
        for crimes against the state,
It's safe for you to now return,
        and holy offer make.
In Power We will show you how
        to work in Pharaoh's field,
But hardened heart will meet you there,
        the pharaoh will not yield." (19)

With wife and sons from desert stay,
        Moses set on the course
For where he'd fled the years before,
        to sing Love Song's decree.
His brother, Aaron, sent by Voice
        to meet him on the trace,
In Horeb's holy shade they met,
        and fell into embrace. (20)

In Egypt, calling elders in,
      they told them of Love's plan.
With staff and hand he showed them signs,
      and sang Love's Song's refrain,
And when, at last, they were convinced ,
      of great I AM's concern,
Of Love's desire to rescue them,
      they worshiped in return. (21)

Pharaoh did shun the faithful two
      who bore the message clear.
With prideful scorn he scorned Love's Song,
      denying them their quest,
And brought great stress upon the slaves
      increasing cruelty's grid.
While Israel's bricks had less the straw,
      the more the prophets bid. (22)

With plagues of snakes, blood, frogs, and gnats,
      with flies, and livestock dead...
With boils, with hail, and locust hoards,
      Love answered Pharaoh's court.
And darkness fell upon the land,
      so thick it could be felt.
The more these prophets were despised,
      the more the curse was dealt. (23)

Pharaoh hardened all the more,
      refused to let them go.
"Out of my sight, do not come back,
      for if you do you'll die."
"Just as you say," Moses replied,
      "We'll not be here again.
Misery will consume your land,
      there's nothing you can gain." (24)

There's one last plague to be invoked
      to mark this history's hour.
Death's angel passing o'er the land,
      all firstborn sons will die.
From Pharaoh's court he'll take the son,
      down to the least one's goat.
This prideful ruler will concede,
      in misery he'll dote. (25)

To Israel, too, this Song is sung,
      for death has no respect.
"Inside the house you'll share a lamb,
      without a blemished spot.
On doorways then with hyssop branch,
      you'll spread the blood thereon.
When I see blood, I'll pass o'er you,
      your firstborn sons atoned. (26)

"And eat no bread that's made with yeast,
     eat all this lamb tonight.
Stand shod with sandals on your feet,
     your cloak tucked in your belt.
And eat this sovereign meal in haste,
     let none of it remain."
The sign was made of this dark night
     to mark a Lamb that's slain. (27)

THE CANTO OF SOJOURN

Not only does the king repent,
    but all the people, too.
All of Egypt recants their pride,
    before the morning breaks.
Gold, silver, clothing from them, too,
    were given as a wage.
The Hebrews left this place with all
    they'd need for the next stage. (1)

Not led in paths along the road,
    but through the desert bare,
Love's Song led Israel's infant band
    toward marshy sea of reeds.
Led by pillar of cloud by day,
    pillar of fire by night,
They were boldly guided out
    into a chartless flight. (2)

But Pharaoh's heart again turned hard,
    for pride despises loss.
He went with chariots and swords
    to meet them at the bog.
With sea in front and wilds aside,
    fear gripped them with its lie,
"'Tis better to be Egypt's slaves,
    than in this desert die." (3)

The Song of Love's a desert song,
    It sings the ways of God.
From cloud they heard Voice say with calm,
    to soothe their restlessness,
"Go raise your staff o'er waters still,
    so they'll be cut in two.
Wind I will send, " the Voice intoned,
    "and I'll deliver you." (4)

The Voice Who led them on the way,
    now came around behind,
Between the army of pursuit
    and the pursued He stood.
The Fire and Cloud took station there;
    it was an awesome sight.
While Wind drove back the waters there,
    It swept throughout the night. (5)

Israel walked into the wash,
      as if in dry ravine.
Then Pharaoh came along the path
      with horse and chariots bold.
Voice ordered utter chaos next,
      and wheels asunder went,
So stayed midst water's rite they were,
      this mighty army spent. (6)

Moses came forth, stretched out his staff
      and let the waters loose.
At daybreak, then, the waters broke
      at their Creator's Word,
Swept forth to cover all the past,
      baptism's awesome wake.
For in the sea and in the cloud,
      the past is given break. (7)

Then on into the desert bare,
      this motley throng were led,
To face the arid wasteland's strain,
      and journey to their goal.
Voice sang to them a simple rule,
      "Listen most carefully,
You must in My Eyes, do what's right,
      then safe and sound you'll be." (8)

The Voice of Love provides for them,
    their every mortal need,
With Cloud by day to shade the heat,
    and Fire by night, the cold,
With manna for their daily bread,
    and quail sent from the Voice.
But, water they'd dependent be
    on Love's directive choice. (9)

Three days into the barren land,
    fresh water did not show.
The people grumbled viciously,
    blamed Moses for their plight.
"What good was gained by coming here,
    only to die of thirst?"
Then Moses cried out to the Voice,
    for Song was being cursed. (10)

"Go to the rock at Horeb's base,
    and I will stand thereon.
Go with your staff and strike the rock
    and water will come forth.
Massah shall now this place be called,
    for you dared test Me there.
Thus, Merebah shall be its name,
    My people quarreled here." (11)

The Song will use this as a sign,
     in generations hence.
This Rock will follow through the land,
     till all may drink therefrom,
To show the Promise will be true,
     life's true foundation sure.
Offense to many He will be,
     and struck to spill the cure. (12)

They soon returned to Horeb's shade,
     Mount Sinai's lofty crag.
From in the Cloud the Voice sang forth,
     and Moses caught the sound,
"In three days hence I'll come to these
     whom I have freed from death.
They must not touch this mount or rim,
     for I'll be in its cleft." (13)

The Lord descended to the peak
     amidst the Smoke and Cloud.
Mid burning Fire, and awesome scene,
     the sound of trumpet blasts.
The Voice gave laws to show them how
     the scales of justice weigh.
These laws were meant to govern them,
     till Voice becomes the Way. (14)

Levites were set as priestly tribe,
     for rites that praise the LORD.
Also a place to worship Them,
     with incense, bread, and lamp.
And holy place of Holy Ones,
     Their glory to intone,
An ark of covenant was there,
     the footstool for the Throne. (15)

With Fire and Cloud and Glory bright,
     the people crossed the plain,
Till Canaan's land they soon arrived,
     the destination made.
For forty days twelve men were sent
     to exploration make,
And brought back news of giants there,
     that they must overtake. (16)

The people cried and wailed dismayed,
     "To Egypt we'll return."
The Voice of Love could not be heard,
     for fear they could not cope.
The enemy of Love is fear,
     which perfect love casts out;
Cold terror froze the hearts that day,
     and panic made the shout. (17)

Though four pled bravely for the LORD,
      their words were swallowed up,
Moses and Aaron were rebuffed...
      Joshua, Caleb shunned.
They must turn back with all the rest,
      to stay with Love's decree.
To rush ahead from under Cloud,
      would seal pride's destiny. (18)

So back into the desert sand,
      the people were to drift,
Till all that came from Egypt's grip,
      were purged from rebel's band.
All, that is, but the faithful ones,
      who trusted in the Song,
And once again, with renewed kin,
      they'd sing with voices strong. (19)

Meandering through desert bare
      their penance to endure,
The people marked their journey's path,
      with ritual and rite.
So feasts and fasts were kept to view
      salvation's history.
Thus, children learned I AM'S Love Song
      by sacred liturgy. (20)

Passover was a special time;
        each year the lessons learned,
Of Israel's bondage and escape,
        by blood their freedom bought.
Such predication honors God
        for all the times of yore,
But, all the more it keeps alive
        the Love Song's sacred score. (21)

They wandered in that desert land,
        returned to Meribah,
That Rock the staff had struck before,
        to give its lode of life.
The people challenged Love again
        to slack their deadly thirst.
"Speak to that Rock," said great I AM,
        "with water it will burst." (22)

Moses was in a ferment now,
        was weary of their threat.
He raised his arm and with his staff
        he struck the Rock again,
Not once, but twice he struck the Rock
        in his intolerance.
The water flowed, their thirst was slacked,
        but Love thus took offense. (23)

The sign of Love was now made lame,
      the Way of Rock was spoiled.
He Whom the world would strike but once
      to give the gift of Love,
That which would purchase holiness,
      a new and living Way.
And Water from the Rock would flow,
      a fount for those who pray. (24)

Moses would never enter now,
      the promised land he sought,
"Because you did not trust in Me
      and give Me honor due,
You will not bring these I have saved
      into the promised land."
The desert song's a Song of Love,
      but love sometimes must ban. (25)

Moses would only viewing make,
      his season had been spent.
No leader since has ever shown
      such awesome, mighty deeds.
No prophet would do like he did,
      and sing with Voice's tone,
'Til Voice Himself would advent make
      to lead to heaven's Throne. (26)

THE CANTO OF DAVID

They crossed the river Jordan first,
    with waters fresh and pure.
The Ark of God they followed through,
    and were baptized anew.
For these had not seen Pow'r of Voice
    as in the sea of reeds,
Had not been cleansed in waters pure,
    and from their fears be freed. (1)

With AlleluYah as their cry,
    the walls before them shook,
And cities fell before the band,
    the land was soon possessed.
But Israel did not cleanse entire,
    impurities retained.
Tainting the love, allowing pride,
    the chosen would be stained. (2)

Trouble would their future be
      for generations yet,
And Voice would have to sing again
      to settle pride's old score.
With judges there would be a way
      for Voice to sing Love's Song,
To guide, instruct, and comfort them,
      and seek to right the wrong. (3)

The last judge, a devoted man,
      was chosen in the womb.
His mother bare, had prayed for child,
      and Love had heard her cause.
She gave him to the LORD in thanks,
      while he was but a boy,
To learn to hear the Voice of Love,
      and faithfully deploy. (4)

The young boy's name was Samuel
      and that means "Name of God,"
So he was raised in Eli's house,
      who was both judge and priest.
And in those days the Ark of God
      was kept in such a place,
The temple cordoned off to form
      the need for holy space. (5)

One night Eli, whose eyes were dimmed,
 had laid his head in sleep.
Samuel could not sleep at all,
 the Lamp of God was lit.
He found the dark, but in the space
 where Holy Ark was kept,
Love's Song then sang to innocence,
 where pride had not yet crept. (6)

For Love's Song is a desert song
 heard simply by a child,
And Samuel thought Eli called,
 and answered, "Here am I."
He ran to Eli's sleeping side
 and said, "I'm here, you called?"
But old Eli denied the claim
 and back Samuel crawled. (7)

Twice more the boy heard Love sing out
 beckoning by his name,
And twice more in child's innocence
 he ran to Eli's bed.
Upon the third, the priest discerned,
 divine intent was clear,
"Go lie down, if Voice repeats, say,
 'Speak, your servant hears.'" (8)

Voice then came in and stood beside
    this child beyond reproach,
And thus He sang as thrice before,
    He called the boy by name.
Samuel in obedience
    rejoined as he was told.
The desert space of innocence
    then heard what Voice extolled. (9)

Voice met Samuel many times,
    and as the boy grew strong,
He was well known by all who heard
    as prophet of the LORD.
He knew the Voice and sang the Song,
    throughout the promised land,
Not one note of the desert Song
    fell from Samuel's hand. (10)

Allowing pagan's set to thrive
    among the chosen race
Would soon give way to profane thought,
    attractions bold and base.
Love's Song rejected as the Way,
    praise was a distant thing,
Like those around them seemed to have,
    pride would require a king. (11)

Samuel sang to Israel,
        Love was their sovereign Head,
But pride had cluttered up the heart,
        and Love would not be heard.
Samuel even plainly sang
        of all a king required,
Yet, they refused the Song of Love,
        for pride wants what's admired. (12)

So Love allowed them their request,
        and Love rejection took.
Voice chose a man named Saul to rule,
        unequaled by the rest.
Saul reigned four score, a warrior bold,
        and slew his thousand foes,
But could not keep the Lord's commands,
        as pride so often goes. (13)

Saul sought to hide his haughtiness,
        with offerings of rams.
Does God delight in offerings
        or in obeying Voice?
Rebellion is as witchcraft done,
        arrogance idol's thing.
The Lord rebuked Saul for his pride,
        rejecting him as king. (14)

A shepherd boy was chosen next,
        the least of Jesse's sons.
A boy who sang with harp in hand,
        whenever Wind would blow.
While in the desert watching sheep,
        he'd sing of Love alone.
David was unctioned secretly
        before he took the throne. (15)

King Saul became depressed and sad,
        though he did not know why.
His close advisors counseled him
        to have a harpist play
When he would melancholy get...
        someone who heard the Voice.
The king agreed, sent scouts about,
        and David was the choice. (16)

So David came to serve the king,
        Saul liked him very much,
And when torment engrossed the king,
        young David played and sang.
Saul's armor bearer he became
        and so was kept close by
To sing the healing words of Love
        and soothe the soul gone dry. (17)

An enemy came with a force
     invading Israel.
There was a standstill on the field,
     the soldiers full of fright.
Opposing them, a giant bold,
     hurled insults vile and base,
And challenged someone from the ranks
     to fight him face to face. (18)

The battle had been stalled all day,
     for no one would be matched.
But David took the challenge up,
     and begged to do the task.
He told of killing lion and bear,
     and soon convinced the king,
Rejecting sword and shield, the lad
     went forth with just a sling. (19)

The giant bellowed and he cursed
     at such an unarmed boy,
"Am I a dog that fears your sticks?
     I'll feed your flesh to birds!"
"You come to fight with sword and spear,
     but I fight in the Name.
The LORD today will strike you down."
     was David's faithful claim. (20)

Then David reached into his bag
      and chose a stone with care,
And hurled it with the sling he had
      with all his strength and might.
It struck the braggart in the head,
      the haughty man fell dead,
And David drew the man's own sword,
      cut off his pride-filled head. (21)

From that day on Saul gave him rank
      to lead the army out.
David triumphed on battle's field
      and in the people's hearts.
They heralded him with song and dance,
      in honor they would spin,
"Saul, his thousands he has slain,
      but David, that, times ten!" (22)

Thus, Saul was filled with jealousy,
      was galled by lost esteem,
And soon the pouting turned to fear,
      recalling Love's rebuke.
He put the youth in battle's front,
      to rid him of the pest,
But more the conflict, more the gain,
      and more pest proved the best. (23)

Envy will rage where pride is fed,
    and turn to hatefulness.
Then hate in turn will plan and scheme,
    just like the fallen star.
David evaded King Saul's wrath,
    into the desert fled,
The valley of death's shadow's chill,
    the place of robber's bed. (24)

Now Love sings a desert song
    to hearts of good intent,
And David soon was asked to lead
    a band of renegades.
King Saul sought David off and on,
    through years of desert life.
But David would not kill the king,
    or be killed in the strife. (25)

David's valor grew greatly there,
    in Love Song's desert den.
He learned the deeper things of Love,
    and set a paradigm.
He learned to chant the Desert Song,
    with words the Wind would bring,
And thus he was prepared by Love,
    redemption's Song to sing. (26)

In time King Saul, the fallen crown,
     would meet his own demise.
With battle lost the man of pride
     would beg to be run through.
When aids refused, Saul by his hand,
     fell on his sword and died.
The enemy cut off his head,
     his honor was denied. (27)

When David heard of King Saul's death,
     he cried out loud and strong,
"How the mighty have now fallen,
     the weapons have all gone."
Though David was begrudged by Saul,
     he loved Saul nonetheless.
In desert harsh love sang a song
     forgiving Saul's duress. (28)

David went up to Judah's tribe,
     and was anointed king.
The Voice ordained him so to be,
     when but a shepherd lad.
Let Love choose the time that is best
     to place the rightful crown.
The song is Love's Song to compose
     for history's redound. (29)

He would lead Judah as a king
      and soon all Jacob's sons,
And bring a heart to Israel
      that sang Love's desert song,
A song of worship, joy, and praise,
      exulting true life-spring
That brings the Ark to its own tent
      in festal gathering. (30)

David's reign was marked with a faith,
      a trust in Love's Song's verse.
The borders of the kingdom's rule
      would be the largest yet.
The heart of David turned to God
      for every judgment made,
So Love's Song sang its song of joy,
      thus David's reign was weighed. (31)

But love itself is different done,
      depending on its course,
And David felt that awesome vibe
      when fair Bathsheba showed.
He took her as kings often do,
      though she was not his own;
He knew this was deceitful pride,
      that Love would not condone. (32)

She with child did soon appear,
     and sent word to the king.
Bathsheba was Uriah's love,
     a man of character.
Her husband was away at war,
     the child could not be his,
So David sent for him to come
     and answer battle quiz. (33)

"Go see your wife while you are home"
     was David's prize to give.
Uriah's valor was his pledge,
     he did not go to her.
"When all my brothers sleep in tents
     on open battlefield,
How can I go home on this night,
     and to temptation yield?" (34)

When David's scheme was thwarted so,
     he suffered from the blame.
By letter David notified
     the leader of the raid,
To place Uriah in the front,
     and leave him there alone.
That's how Bathsheba's husband died,
     how sin became full blown. (35)

"So pride doth go before the fall,"
  the proverb rings its truth,
From pride, desire, guile, then fraud,
  and so the web is spun.
His throne, his sons, and Isra'l, too,
  would suffer for this wrong.
From Eden's shade to Judah's halls,
  self sings its dreadful song. (36)

When this child's time had fully come,
  the bairn was in death's throes,
The father mourned and prayed for days
  till babe in stillness lay.
Bathsheba then became his wife;
  he loved her all the more.
For more the pride is known to hurt,
  the more doth love restore. (37)

But errors done in desert times
  are hardest to conceal,
And by his sin he had exposed
  his sons to pride and greed.
His sons rebelled and tore his heart;
  the desert had returned,
A sadness played on David's harp,
  his heart's remorse would churn. (38)

From Israel came chosen ones,
      from Judah came the tribe,
From David comes one full of grace,
      through whom all lives are blessed.
But prideful ways and selfish thoughts
      among life's wheat are tares,
Yet, Love's Song is a faithful song,
      and will the breach repair. (33)

CANTO OF THE PROPHETS

The kings that followed David's reign,
    did not his songs resound,
And regency of loving heart
    did not the people bless.
The Voice that sung in David's songs,
    was given a deaf ear,
And kings were thus no longer sought,
    to sing the Love Song clear. (1)

The desert of the lack of faith,
    the wilderness of sin,
Were soon the parch that seemed to cast
    aridity about.
But, Love's Song is a desert song,
    and love must resonate;
Thus prophets were the next to see
    what Love articulates. (2)

These men were called from common folk,
      and from the priests as well,
To give the kings awakenings
      and populace the dream.
For Seers see the words of Voice,
      and pass on what they see,
So Love will sing the Promises
      to their posterity. (3)

Moses was a prophet of God
      who led the chosen race,
Who in the promised land were led
      by power, voice, and wind.
But kings would come and kings would go,
      and kings would want it all.
Kings took pride in their own wit,
      and greed was their downfall. (4)

Egypt's bondage had been broken,
      the people had been freed,
But now the sinfulness of kings
      had made them slaves again.
The promised land they had achieved,
      a place of wine and wheat,
But without Water from above,
      it turned to desert heat. (5)

Two kings reject Love's oversight,
    led by their own desires.
The kingdom rent that David built,
    by sons of his own son.
Divided by their jealous pride,
    the northern tribes were ten,
While Judah to the South remained,
    and also Benjamin. (6)

Now who would sing the Song of Love?
    Who would chant with the Wind?
Who could They trust with Words of Love?
    Who would Voice call to sing
Love's Song in such a time as this,
    in desert so arrayed,
With wilderness that's made of pride
    and spiritual decay? (7)

Elijah was among the first
    to see the Voice of Love,
Called to the desert to proclaim
    the famine on the land.
King Ahab was profanity,
    and Jezebel was worse.
It's in their time Elijah came
    to challenge their vile curse. (8)

Jezebel worshipped baals of stone,
    and Ahab lost his way,
While on Mount Carmel near the sea,
    a broken altar lay.
Elijah challenged prophets there,
    eight hundred fifty strong,
"If the LORD is God, follow Him…
    if baal be god, I'm wrong. (9)

"Prepare your god a holocaust,
    but do not light the fire;
Beseech your baal to give forth fire,
    and prove that he's a god."
The prophets called out mightily,
    from morning until eve,
But there's no answer for their cries,
    for they had been deceived. (10)

Elijah took twelve stones aside
    and brought the people round.
He then rebuilt the altar there
    so Love would have a stage.
Then wood was laid, a trench was dug
    encircling the place.
The sacrifice was laid thereon
    and thrice the water laced. (11)

At time of evening sacrifice,
        Elijah sang to Love.
The Fire of God fell from above,
        burned water, stones, and wood.
The people's hearts turned back to Them,
        as they all prostrate fell.
"I AM is God, He truly is!"
        in penance was their knell. (12)

The prophets that were false were seized,
        brought down from there and killed.
As rain began that had not been,
        King Ahab turned for home.
When Jezebel heard of this plight,
        she swore Elijah's fate.
And put a warrant on his head,
        that he would taste her hate. (13)

Elijah then was gripped with fear
        and ran away in haste,
And walked that day in desert waste,
        for he had had enough.
"Now take my life, for I'm no good,"
        he begged and fell asleep,
But Love knew him and Voice called out,
        "A journey you must keep." (14)

Voice fed him there and led him on
        to desert deep and bare,
For Love's Song is a desert song
        and heard best when alone.
To Horeb's ancient site he went,
        where Moses faced the LORD,
And there he went into a cave
        to hear Love's simple chord. (15)

"Your Name I have defended, LORD,
        your covenant and law.
Your altars they have broken down,
        your prophets have been killed.
Now I, I only have been left,
        to do too much for one,"
Elijah made his case to Love,
        of all that he had done. (16)

"Go out and stand on mountain's ledge,
        for I will pass you by."
Voice urged Elijah to commit
        to know of Presence true.
The desert's bare and hot and sparse,
        and one can feel outcast.
When one thus feels he most is true,
        in desert he is last. (17)

A mighty wind tore rocks apart,
　　　but Presence was not there.
An earthquake then shook Horeb's base,
　　　but Presence was not seen.
Then scorching fire seared all around,
　　　but Presence's not in sight.
Elijah heard a gentle Breath,
　　　and hid his face in fright. (18)

Love's Song has such a unique tone,
　　　Elijah knew the Voice,
"Now go back there and serve me still,
　　　and sing of promise true,
For seven thousand have not knelt
　　　nor kissed the mouth of stone."
So Voice thus sang the desert song,
　　　Elijah's not alone. (19)

Elijah stayed to sing for God,
　　　of all the prophet saw.
He lent his voice to sing the Song,
　　　as moved upon by Voice.
His word and works were legend made,
　　　his faith exemplary,
For desert song had weaved its grace
　　　in one whom Truth set free. (20)

So faithful and courageous he,
      that he would not taste death,
The very thing that he feared most,
      and to the desert fled.
Assumed one day in Wind and Fire,
      the chariot of Grace,
Elijah's life of piety
      earned him celestial place. (21)

Tradition rose among God's race,
      Elijah would return,
Like Moses, taken by the LORD,
      He, too, escaped the grave.
"To you I'll send Elijah strong,"
      the Voice will one day sing.
As Truth's precursor he will be,
      Love's Song will he then bring. (22)

Elisha was the Voice's choice,
      Elijah to succeed.
Apprenticed to Elijah's side,
      a farmer called to see.
When time drew nigh for Them to take
      Elijah in the Wind,
Elisha stayed and walked with him
      to face what They would send. (23)

"Let me have twice your spirit's share,"
        Elisha did request.
"If you see me when I must go,
        the double you will have."
Suddenly the chariot came
        with horses all afire!
Elijah went up then and there;
        Elisha stared in fright. (24)

The cloak Elijah wore that day,
        the mantle of his pow'r,
Had fluttered back onto the ground;
        Elisha took it up.
The prophet's spirit thus came down
        upon his son of love.
Elisha now would sing the Song
        with visions strained thereof. (25)

Elisha's exploits with the LORD
        were signs for Love's great Song.
Waters are cured and food made whole,
        the dead restored to life,
Multitudes fed and lepers healed,
        and widow given son,
With waters gushed upon dry ground;
        all signs of One to come. (26)

Yes, Love's Song is a desert song,
      Elisha sang it well.
For in the court and battlefield,
      or private residence,
Elisha's cadences were felt
      throughout that desert land.
This seer saw and what he saw
      became Love's tonic strand. (27)

There was a time that Israel,
      the ten tribes to the north,
Received Love's Song in short descants,
      sung true by men of grit.
Love raised them up in troubled times,
      with solos as it were,
And through them Love could sing Their song,
      to love's vain perverter. (28)

First was Micaiah ben Imla,
      a seer of the Voice,
He's called upon the scene but once,
      to render prophecy.
Israel was three years at peace,
      but Ahab chose a fight
To take back land lost to Aram,
      a town among the heights. (29)

Jehoshaphat came down to see
    the king of Israel,
Who quickly asked if he would join
    in prideful battle siege.
Jehoshaphat, not quick to act,
    answered the king's request,
"Let's seek the counsel of the LORD",
    then we'll discern what's best. (30)

So Israel's king called his pride,
    four hundred prophets false,
Who answered "go" when asked what's best,
    "they'll fall into your hand."
But Judah's king did not buy this;
    it lacked sincerity.
These base pretenders served their king
    with false delivery. (31)

A desert was created there,
    a place parched by false gods.
The king in pride had oft forsook
    the leading of the LORD.
Love's faithful Song's a desert song,
    its melody is rich,
But Love could not get through to him,
    for they had been bewitched. (32)

"Is there no prophet of the LORD?"
        Jehoshaphat inquired.
        "Oh, there's this one who sings the Voice,
        but I do hate him sore,
For when he speaks of me these days,
        it's constantly all bad."
Macaiah was the man of faith,
        who made the king so mad. (33)

That day the prophet of the LORD
        was brought before the king,
"Against the ones who stole our land,
        shall we put up a siege
At Ramoth Giliad today,
        or shall we hold our bid?"
Micaiah sensed the king's intent,
        and knew the answer hid. (34)

He mocked the king's four hundred men,
        with irony he quipped,
"Attack and be victorious,"
        he in derision said.
"How many times must I tell you
        to speak to me the truth?!"
Israel's king cried in disgust,
        he sensed Micaiah's couth. (36)

Micaiah then sang to the kings,
      that they'd most surely lose.
He told of how the men of war
      would scatter o'er the hills,
Because of how this king would be
      no longer in the fray,
And loss of heart and courage bold,
      would be their meat that day. (36)

"Did I not tell you of this man,
      that he says nothing good?"
"You'll soon find out if it's the truth,"
      the seer simply said.
"I'll deal with you when I return,"
      the king said in his pride.
"If you return, this word's not true"
      was wise Micaiah's chide. (37)

The kings went forth to seize the heights,
      to test the Voice and Song.
"So you must wear your royal robes,
      and I'll be in disguise,"
The prideful king told Judah's liege...
      did he believe God's man?
A random arrow pierced him through;
      he died despite his plan. (38)

There were true prophets of the LORD,
        called forth but for a flash,
But they give insight to the Song
        that all true seers sing:
That pride is man's most fatal trap,
        from Eden to time's end.
Humility and lowliness
        will be pride's fatal blend. (39)

There was Amos of Tekoa,
        a simple shepherd bold,
Another prophet of the north,
        to render judgment's course.
Where Love warned of a doom to come,
        but also of the hope
That was in store for those who heard
        the Song of Love's true scope. (40)

Hosea, too, from Israel,
        sang strangely of God's love,
"Take for yourself a prostitute,
        and with her children bear,
For you will be a sign for all
        to see their sinfulness.
Israel I have truly loved,
        but they in pride digress. (41)

"Each time your wife the harlot plays,"
     Love's Song went on to sing,
"Is like the times the one I love
     commits idolatry.
Each time you go and bring her back,
     are signs where I attend.
She's sown the wind in sinful pride,
     but now reaped the whirlwind." (42)

These prophets in meek faith complied,
     and bore a message strong,
To those who walked by their own wit
     they tried to sing the Song.
For those of pride and self-respect,
     there was no music heard.
Assyria felled Israel,
     the wrath of Love incurred. (43)

From slaves in Egypt they had come,
     with hope of a new life.
To slavery they now returned,
     for lack of love maintained.
But, Love's Song is a desert song,
     and there they must remain,
Till once again they hear Love's Voice
     to woo them back again. (44)

A prophet of the royal courts
        of four of Judah's kings,
Isaiah, son of Amoz, saw
        the Voice of sacred scheme.
He warned of judgment yet to come,
        but also comfort gave.
He clashed with kings that pride entrapped,
        and sang of One who'll save. (45)

For Love's Song is a desert song,
        Isaiah knew full well,
And Judah had become parched place,
        without the Well of Love.
He used the concept artfully,
        as prompted by the LORD,
And through such desert imagery,
        would faithfully record. (46)

True desolation comes about
        when in the heart of man
No song is sung of life and love,
        no waters are poured forth.
With snakes and thorns, where owls are heard,
        it is a pathless waste,
Without the fertile song of Love,
        a wilderness is faced. (47)

In his divine commissioning,
      in presence of the Three,
He's told that ruin comes about
      because of ignorant bliss.
For "With their ears, they will not hear,
      and seeing, will not see.
And everything will be laid waste,
      but Jesse's Holy Seed." (48)

"So who will go for Us", Voice asked,
      "And who will sing the Song?"
In face of such rejecting ban,
      Isaiah took the call.
Oh, "Here am I. Send me," he said.
      He knew the task was dire.
Isaiah went forth from Their Throne,
      cleansed by the Holy Fire. (49)

The seer sees what Voice doth say,
      and speaks the vision true,
And what Isaiah saw to come,
      made him cry out the more.
"The earth defiled, withers away,
      and gaiety's a lie,
The joyful harp is silent now,
      the wineskin has gone dry. (50)

"The noisy city's silent now,
     the citadel laid waste,
Till Spirit pours on us again,
     till fertile Seed appears,
Till justice dwells in desert wild,
     and righteousness brings peace,
The desert song will be what's sung
     to bring Love's sweet release. (51)

"Our righteous acts are filthy rags;
     we are thus all unclean.
As leaves upon the desert sand,
     our sins sweep us away."
So the prophet sang forth the dirge,
     with sad and dreary tone,
And looked to see Love sing the Song,
     so he'd not sing alone. (52)

Love's Song is still a desert song,
     and They began to sing,
"The desert will rejoice and bloom,
     the wilderness be glad,
A remnant shall return one day
     to Zion's desert land.
There'll be streams in the desert bare,
     and mutes will sing what's planned." (53)

The Song of Love's a song of hope,
     and sings of promises,
Of desert voice to make the way
     for glory to reveal
A highway only for the clean,
     a Way of Holiness,
The ransomed will return on it,
     and crowns of joy possess. (54)

Of virgin birth, the song would sing,
     of an Immanuel,
Of David's throne to be made sure
     for all eternity.
A Child is born, a Son is giv'n,
     and Wonderful is He,
The mighty God and Prince of Peace,
     to set the people free. (55)

In desert bare the trees are cut
     and only stumps remain.
The stump of Jesse bears a shoot;
     the Song would be in Him.
By justice He will judge the poor,
     and right shall be His belt,
With mouth divine He'll strike the earth;
     His breath shall evil melt. (56)

The kingdom He'll establish then,
    will be one full of peace.
The wolf will with the lamb lie down,
    the child with adder play,
The lion and the bear will feed
    and all will be carefree,
And fullness of the LORD be known,
    as waters fill the sea. (57)

As in the time that was not time,
    He'll do this with His Word.
The Voice will speak with Holy Breath,
    to preach love to the poor,
To bind the broken, free those held,
    and comfort all who mourn.
The oil of gladness He will give,
    and lasting praise be worn. (58)

But, this can't happen without cost,
    Their likeness must be saved,
And saved by love is Love Song's quest,
    'tis how Their Arm is shown.
Despised He'll be, rejected, too,
    and pierced for Adam's sin.
So, He is crushed by all the pride
    that's caused the fall of men. (59)

Isaiah was a paradigm
      for prophets new and old.
The seer sees and what he sees
      makes him intone Love's Song
Of what's to come beyond the veil,
      and far beyond his time,
To gaze upon fulfillment blest,
      of mystery sublime. (60)

The prophet Micah, country man,
      a synthesis that's odd,
With absolute destruction sure
      and promises of love.
"Woe to the rich who in self-love,
      plan well their evil wrong.
The LORD the lame will then call forth,
      to drive away the strong. (61)

"Jerusalem will be a heap
      of rubble in the dust.
The temple mount will overgrow
      with thickets of the wild.
The Word from Zion will go forth,
      and from Jerusalem,
And He will teach us of His Way,
      and we will walk with Him." (62)

Such contrasts in the prophecies
        were clearly Micah's mark,
For though Love Song's a desert song,
        'tis still a song of love.
Love seeks the good, but hates the bad,
        so Love casts evil out,
Then fills the loved with Love's own means,
        thus, to remove all doubt. (63)

The casting out of what's not right
        creates a desert place,
And there most often in the dry,
        Love's Song can reach the heart.
Pride crowns the heart with lies of self,
        deceives the darkened mind,
Love is the remedy divine
        to heal the heart that's blind. (64)

Now love's fruit is humility,
        as Micah seemed to know.
For Micah saw what Love Song sang,
        a true and humble way.
"Oh, Bethlehem, though you are small
        among all Judah's clans,
From you shall come the One who rules,
        fulfillment of the plan." (65)

Three other prophets saw the Word
     and warned Jerusalem.
Zephaniah attacked the sins,
     Nahum strikes Nineveh.
Habbakkuk warned of pride and greed,
     oppressions dreadful wrong.
All of these sins a desert makes,
     a place to sing Love's Song. (66)

Cult superstitions, priestly wrongs,
     indulgence for the sin,
Good Zephaniah harshly cries,
     "The Day of I AM comes"!
Humility will sing Love's Song,
     for pride will be denounced,
The remnant will be purified
     the LORD'S truth be announced. (67)

The decimation seen by him,
     of those who make the waste,
Is Nahum's way of filling out
     the vestige of his time.
Conquerors all will fall away,
     the guilty will be doomed,
Woe to the city full of lies,
     from which the pride is hewn. (68)

"How long, O LORD, must I call out?"
   ...Habakkuk's plaintive song,
"Of violent oppression made,
      of justice paralyzed?"
But know the righteous will survive,
      be saved from the abyss.
Ev'n with the wicked, faithless ones,
      Love will accomplish this. (69)

For Love's Song is a desert song,
      and when there's most the need,
All in the world are in the Song
      to bring about the truth.
Three prophets saw what they would sing,
      and did it faithfully,
So Love could move through portal clear,
      to claim the destiny. (70)

Jeremiah would soon be called,
      to sing the sad refrain,
To see the Word and voice the dirge.
      to sing Love Song's lament.
"Before your birth, you were so called,"
      to sing what love's about.
"What do you see?" "A boiling pot."
      "Disaster is poured out." (71)

In wilderness of sinful pride,
      the desert had encroached.
The song of Love was rarely heard;
      the noise of lust sufficed.
The fathers ate their sour grapes,
      put children's teeth on edge.
The prophets lie; the priests are vile,
      for treasure is the pledge. (72)

Faithless Israel to the north
      became the captor's prey.
Now Judah on the scale is thrust
      and weighed against the Love,
For Love would sing the desert song,
      to woo and to attract,
But, love betrayed, once love's been known,
      will loose its usual tack. (73)

Two sins against the Love were dealt,
      that brought the desert in,
"They have refused, forsaken Me,
      the spring of Water's Life,
And dug dry cisterns of their own,
      which cannot hold the rain."
Rejecting Love's Song is the choice
      that leaves the heart profane. (74)

True Love's sweet song a dirge became,
     for Love had been refused,
And sadness comes when Love must deal
     most harshly with the loved.
When Jeremiah heard the moan
     of unrequited love,
With lamentation sadly toned
     the misery thereof. (75)

But those who heard would not atone,
     the love dismissed as fake.
The disbelief began to loathe
     the prophet and the song.
Soon hatred seeped into their hearts,
     and clamored for his life.
The journey into abandon
     was ending in such strife. (76)

Where primordial paradise
     had witnessed Adam's fall,
Was now a curse to all the world,
     the pagan Babylon.
Love called on curse to be a curse,
     to bring about the fall,
And carry into desert land,
     their failure to recall. (77)

Brought up from Egypt's slavery,
      through wilderness of sin,
Turned to slavery's chain again,
      displaced, disgraced, distained.
So sometimes love must push away
      so loved can know what's wrong,
And come to know the mystery
      for which the heart doth long. (78)

Love's Song is still a desert song,
      and gives the vanquished hope.
When Love has had to withhold grace,
      affection does not fade.
Though Babylon's grounds were renown,
      its gold and silver glared,
It was a desert of the soul,
      a place that pride had snared. (79)

Love's Song must sometimes part the course;
      its motif take new turn.
They found a voice to sing the part,
      reminding loved of Love.
Ezekiel saw the vision clear,
      and saw the four vanguards
Who stand around the throne of God,
      so fearful to regard. (80)

Ezekiel saw the wheel in wheel,
     and seraph faces four,
Of man, eagle, lion and ox,
     as if they were on fire.
And Voice sang from above it all,
     with brilliant radiance,
Ezekiel knew Who he heard,
     and fell in holy stance. (81)

"Son of man, I AM sending you
     to rebels obstinate,
To show them what rejection brings
     and where it's sure to lead.
You'll have to go through briars and thorns,
     amidst the scorpions.
Some will listen and some will not,
     but do not be undone." (82)

Ezekiel sang bitter verse
     with pageants to perform.
Conducting was the Holy Voice,
     a fugue that seemed deranged.
Jerusalem's siege was the first,
     in tragedy portrayed.
To show how pride and arrogance
     had caused their love to fade. (83)

Next the exile would be played out
       to this rebellious lot,
To make it clear where they once were,
       and show them what's to come.
They cannot whitewash walls of sin;
       denial was exposed,
And Judgment brings a wilderness
       for faithlessness reposed. (84)

Yes, Love's Song is a desert song
       and oft is an appeal.
This prophet seemed quite mad to all
       with history's revue.
But, in the desert love is heard
       where purged hearts often burn,
And love removes rebellious pride,
       and promises return. (85)

To such a desert plain he's brought,
       a valley of dry bones,
"Man, prophesy to these dry bones
       to hear the Voice of God,
Say to them, 'Receive your flesh,
       and breathe the Breath anew,
For hope's not gone, though you're cut off,
       by Spirit they'll be true.'" (86)

So, thus the remnant shall return,
    though first to Love with faith.
As in the days when Moses led
    through desert waste reviewed,
A remnant of the former clan
    will see the promised land.
The glory of the LORD will fill
    the temple once again. (87)

Young Daniel was of noble birth
    when taken from his home.
He came to the attention of
    the court of Babylon.
Daniel and three of his best friends
    were groomed in royal ways,
Much because of their comely looks
    and grace that they conveyed. (88)

The king of Babylon had dreams;
    his sorcerers were called.
The challenge that was put to them,
    Was "know the dream entire"!
They could not meet the king's demand
    and faced the scimitar,
But Daniel, known for wisdom pure,
    would come and clear the mar. (89)

"A statue great and fearsome stood,
     with head made of pure gold,
With silver for its chest and arms,
     and awesome to behold.
The belly and the thighs were bronze,
     with legs of iron arrayed,
And both its feet were made of iron
     that's mixed with miry clay. (90)

"While you watched this, a rock was cut,
     but not by human hands.
It struck the statue on the feet,
     and all the rest came down.
The image was reduced to dust,
     which Wind would blow away.
The rock became a mountain huge;
     the entire earth displayed. (91)

"So that, O king, was your great dream,
     I'll tell you what it means.
The head of gold is you, O king,
     the breast, the next monarch;
A third kingdom, this one of bronze,
     will rule o'er all the earth.
And finally there will arise
     a fourth with iron its girth. (92)

"Iron breaks in pieces all the rest,
        but feet and toes were mixed
With clay that makes for brittleness,
        and cleaves not to itself.
Two legs of iron means it will be
        divided east and west,
With people mixed and unconformed,
        no single pow'r to vest. (93)

"As to the rock cut without hands,
        God will thus intervene,
A kingdom indestructible,
        not left for conquering.
The rock was cut out without hands,
        a rock to crush all things.
The dream is true, what God has shown,
        to you O king of kings." (94)

What Daniel saw was time laid out,
        the kingdoms who would come.
History tells us what then took place,
        and played out after that:
Assyria fell Babylon,
        then Macedon would reign.
Next, there'd arise on seven hills
        the cult of Rome's domain. (95)

What Daniel saw in the king's dream,
      the Song of Love will sing:
In quietness Love will supply
      the Kingdom born of grace.
And in the days of Rome would be
      the Way Truth would employ.
What Love had sung since before time
      will be good news of joy. (96)

THE DESERT DANCE

CANTO OF THE SON OF GOD

The desert song is mystery,
      kept hidden in the past,
But mystery in sacred song's
      disclosed by promise made.
All types and shadows of Love's acts
      have built the rapture sweet,
And brought the beloved to relish
      anticipation reached. (1)

In the fullness of all these times
      in which Love Song was sung,
There came a time the mystery
      should be made fully known.
The promise made means promise kept
      when made by Voice that's True.
The moment's here for Love Themselves to
      Dance for all to view. (2)

Disclosure of the heart of Love
      most often seeks surprise,
And joys in the astonishment,
      of Their beloved's awe.
Seers had said the Dance would come,
      but who had thought like this?
The Prophet, Priest, and King, as one,
      would dance within our midst. (3)

The Word by which all things were made,
      that gave identity,
The Voice by which Love Song was known,
      that came to Adam's aid,
Who stayed the knife of Abraham,
      son's sacrifice declined.
The Rock from Whom the water flowed,
      Manna for those who dined. (4)

Who from burning bush disclosed
      the Name, the great I AM,
The Light and Life of all mankind,
      be at this time displayed.
The time had come for Song's climax,
      a Way for all to know,
This dance is but the joy of Love,
      the step for Lead to show. (5)

All that's been until now portrayed,
     has been to form the dance,
And bring to fullness all of time,
     that's used by Love as scale.
Again, 'tis set in desert made
     from pride's audacity.
In Rome no greater boast's been made,
     than claim divinity. (6)

In those dark days of ruthless reign,
     in desert of duress,
When Herod of Judea ruled,
     but as a puppet king,
A faithful priest served worshippers,
     Zechariah by name.
An angel of the Lord appeared
     amidst the incense flame. (7)

"Fear not, O faithful one, fear not,
     your prayer for child is heard.
A son Elizabeth will bear,
     and you will name him, John.
A delightful joy he will be,
     and many will be awed;
Elijah's spirit he will own
     to pave the way for God." (8)

Zechariah could not compose
       the angel's aria.
Could what he saw be really there,
       could what is sung be true?
Elizabeth, beyond the years,
       as Sarah was of old.
His faithfulness would falter here;
       the disbelief would show. (9)

"For I am Gabriel who stands
       at the throne of the LORD,"
Who's seen the Song of Love sung from
       before then until now.
The Song of Love's a desert song,
       sung both in word and deed,
In deserts made from pride and doubt,
       but heard by ears of need. (10)

Rome had so made a desert bare
       of faith and hope and love.
And Herod's throne a desert void
       of joy and righteousness.
"You'll be silent until the day
       that all this comes about."
With angel voice a desert's made
       of Zechariah's doubt. (11)

The silence of the desert is,
        for one whose been therein,
A place where many thoughts collide,
        where will and conscience blend.
Till thought and will, along with soul,
        is muted by the heart,
And Love can sing of love to one
        whose pride will not distort. (12)

'Twas such a one in quietness
        of Naz'reth's little town
One meek and lowly, self-abased,
        with holy life portrayed.
The angel came to sing to her,
        sent from her LORD above,
To sing Their Word to her young heart,
        with tenderness and love. (13)

To her, "Hail Mary, full of grace,"
        the angel signified.
"The Lord is with you even now,"
        he sang to her pure heart.
But, Mary trembled at his words;
        they were too high for her.
"Fear not for favor you have found,"
        Gabriel did aver. (14)

"With child you'll be, a son you'll give,
    his name shall Jesus be.
He will be great, the Son of God,
    the throne of David take.
He'll reign for'er o'er Jacob's House,
    His kingdom will not end."
The virgin knew what these words meant,
    what Love Song did portend. (15)

"How will this be, I know no man,
    how will this all take place?"
She dared to ask in simple tone,
    in wonder, yet in trust.
"The Holy Spirit will descend
    envelope you in love.
The One who will be born of this
    is Son of God above. (16)

"Elizabeth, your relative,
    whose barrenness is broke,
Is now in her sixth month reposed,
    for nothing's beyond God."
Not understanding angels' words,
    she knew this was the Word,
"Behold the handmaid of the Lord,
    may it be done as heard." (21)

So now in time, Voice who brought forth
      all of creation's works,
Would come to be a tiny Spot
      in this untarnished womb.
The One who walked in garden bleak,
      when woman fell to pride,
Now will by woman be brought forth,
      indwelling flesh abide. (18)

The blessed virgin has conceived,
      the sign the prophet saw.
His name would be Immanuel,
      "God with us" now in time.
The Song of Love quietly sung,
      passion quietly felt,
For Word would come most tenderly
      as mystery is dealt. (19)

Then Mary hurried from that place
      to greet Elizabeth,
To sing the Song the angel sang,
      to comfort her with joy.
At Mary's word, the baby leaped
      in older woman's womb.
At that Elizabeth was filled,
      the Breath of God assumed. (20)

"Blessed are you among women!"
      Elizabeth exclaimed.
"Blessed be the Fruit of your womb,
      why am I favored so?
The blessed mother of my Lord
      to come and visit me?
You have believed when Word was sung,
      that it for sure would be." (21)

Eternal Word's the pow'r by which
      all that's done is done.
The light and life came by that Might,
      accomplishing what's sung.
For Breath puts spirit on the words,
      to give them meaning due,
And Love's design acquires its end,
      its color and its hue. (22)

Now, she in whom Word's been infleshed,
      takes up the sweet descant,
"My soul doth magnify the Lord,
      my spirit's filled with joy.
God, my Savior, made known of me,
      His servant-girl professed,
And generations yet to come,
      will laud my blessedness. (23)

"The Mighty One's done great by me,
　　and holy is His Name.
His mercy and His Song of Love
　　extends from ages past.
He has torn down all haughtiness,
　　and lifted up the poor,
And filled the hungry with good things,
　　made rich an empty sore. (24)

"He's helped beloved Israel,
　　and kept His promise made,
To come to this, He's sung His Song
　　as faithful through and through."
Staying through Elizabeth's time,
　　sweet Mary served her needs.
Returning home, she faced the scorn,
　　the suspect of foul deed. (25)

Mary to Joseph was betrothed,
　　a good and kindly man.
Unwilling to disgrace his love,
　　in sad confusion lay.
The angel of the Lord appeared
　　to Joseph in a dream,
And gave poor Joseph confidence,
　　revealing Love Song's scheme. (26)

Now Joseph was a faithful man,
     who took young Mary in,
To be her husband, she his wife,
     but did not consummate.
For he now knew his life would be
     guardian of the King.
He must stand strong o'er these so blest
     and help Salvation sing. (27)

When Mary's time drew near to birth
     the Promise of God's love,
In pride, Augustus set a count
     of all the world of Rome.
Each to the town of family line,
     the edict would declare,
So Joseph went to Bethlehem,
     for David was forbear. (28)

The prophet saw in ancient times,
     a ruler would come forth.
For Bethlehem, the smallest clan,
     will host the labor there.
When Joseph came 'twas Mary's time,
     no room was there for rent;
The inns were filled, the stables, too,
     where traveling stock is pent. (29)

At village edge, a grotto's found,
    and it will have to do,
For 'tis the night of urgency
    of woman's greatest need,
No bed, no water for her stress,
    no mid-wife's gentle stead,
No door to guard life's sacrament,
    no place to lay Babe's head. (30)

For Love's Song is a desert song,
    in places stark and bare,
'Cause in such Love can be most known,
    un-dazzled by the best.
A virgin birth, an unskilled man,
    no light except the moon,
She thus brought forth her newborn Son
    to Love's celestial tune. (31)

She swaddled Him with loving hands,
    then laid in manger near.
A feeding trough carved in the stone
    was there for Him to sleep.
She rested with contentment then,
    exhausted to opine.
Her Baby came when Love was due,
    the Hope of all mankind. (32)

The King of kings had just been born,
　　　　but not in palace halls,
Nor were the priests or rabbis there
　　　　for prophecy revealed.
Event from which all time is scored,
　　　　yet shroud of mystery,
Begotten of the great I AM
　　　　in holy poverty. (33)

Bethlehem was a modest place,
　　　　with shepherds fields about,
And watching sheep in nearby space
　　　　were those who kept the flock.
They're simple and unlearned folk,
　　　　the poorest of the poor,
The kind who've always had Love's heart,
　　　　the ones who rich ignore. (34)

For Love's Song is a desert song
　　　　the poor in spirit hear.
An angel of the Lord appeared
　　　　to sing the wondrous verse:
"Good news! Great joy I bring to you,"
　　　　the angel sang to them.
"Christ, the Lord has been born this day,
　　　　in nearby Bethlehem." (35)

With glory bright, the heavens rent,
    angelic chorus sang,
"Glory to God in the highest,
    to all men peace on earth."
Terrified, yet with wonder filled,
    the shepherds heard the news,
And hurried off to find the child,
    as simple poor would do. (36)

They found the child as they were told,
    Life wrapped in manger stone.
What awesome sign of things to come,
    (Life shrouded in a tomb).
They did not know, had no idea,
    that they were seers stirred.
Did they respond in years beyond
    to resurrection's word? (37)

Now, Love's Song is a desert song,
    and oft deposit's made
In barren lives to not distract
    in complicated ways.
Mystery's stored inside the poor,
    to sing as time doth sort,
And Mary, too, did treasure all
    these things within her heart. (38)

Hebrew born under Hebrew law,
        the couple would comply
To rites of birth as were prescribed,
        so circumcised and named.
Then, Mary must submit in time,
        to pur'fication test,
And consecrate this firstborn male
        to God as code expressed. (39)

While in the place of sacrifice,
        a devout, holy man,
Who, Spirit filled, he had been told,
        he'd see Love's Song fulfilled.
Old Simeon observed the child,
        and took Him in his arms,
"My eyes have seen Salvation now,
        for all whom sin has harmed." (40)

Joseph and Mary marveled there
        for what was said of Him,
"The fall and rising He'll impart;
        this Child will be a sign.
The thoughts of hearts will be revealed;
        a sword will pierce your soul."
O Mystery, O Love exposed,
        what wonder to extol? (41)

As time went by, they found a place
        to live while Joseph worked,
For he had not been led of Love,
        to leave meek Bethlehem.
When Christ was born, a star appeared,
        in night sky of the east.
To magi learned in such things,
        it was divine release. (42)

Often, because it's out of sight,
        it is forgot by most,
That Love has others in this world
        who've come to know His light.
O Mystery, what's often hid,
        like great Melchizedek,
Love uses in this sacred Song,
        to keep the tune in check. (43)

So with their knowing of what's meant,
        of sacred unknown source,
These men of bearing set their course,
        by yonder star aligned.
It led them to Jerusalem,
        where pride ruled on the throne,
For they assumed that all would know,
        just why the star had shone. (44)

So in the halls of royalty,
     they searched for such a babe,
But found instead a king alarmed
     at news of such a birth.
Herod, in fearful arrogance,
     had murdered all who might
Usurp his throne, as old Ahaz,
     when this birth came to light. (45)

This king was Idumean born,
     he had usurped this throne,
So his great fear was that the same
     would end his sad career.
Through the chief priests, he found the key
     to magi's search unknown,
That Bethlehem would birth the king
     that takes Davidic throne. (46)

Then Herod learned from these wise men
     the time the star appeared,
And sent them on to Bethlehem
     to find the newborn King.
"Search for this child and when you're done,
     come and report to me,
That I may come to Bethlehem,
     and worship him with thee." (47)

The star drew them to journey's end,
    to humble Bethlehem.
Divergent brightness glory bend,
    the men could plainly see
Until at last they came to stand,
    with expectation's grace,
With hearts aflame they stood in awe
    of peasant dwelling place. (48)

Had magi known the Love Song's theme,
    they would not be surprised,
For it's a desert song that's sung,
    from all eternity.
The King they sought would only be
    One seen by modest eyes,
There in the door an infant child
    in star-beam amplified. (49)

The men of East without a word,
    fell faces to the ground,
Worshiped the Child, this Holy One,
    whose advent heaven claimed.
Epiphany, the flash of light,
    that revelation gives,
It is for all whom sin doth blight,
    who in its desert lives. (50)

With gifts of gold, myrrh, frankincense,
      they gave the Child His due,
Not knowing that they'd be required
      for holy family's need.
For now Love's Song would give alert
      to Joseph in a dream,
That Herod soon would take the hunt,
      and loose a bloody scheme. (51)

The magi, though, were warned in sleep,
      to leave another way,
That Herod's plan to kill the Child
      would so unaided be.
When evil deeds are thwarted thus,
      the fury can't abide,
And Herod would be known through time,
      for sick infanticide. (52)

As Rachel wept for children lost,
      so town of Bethlehem,
The wailing of the mothers there,
      no comfort could be given.
As son of Ahaz was redeemed,
      from father's jealousy,
The Son of God is secreted
      from Herod's vile decree. (53)

'Tis odd to note that when there's hope
      of life in godly state,
It's children in the womb or out,
      who pay the price of hate.
When pride is probed by heaven's light,
      it strikes out viciously
Against those who have no defense,
      aborting destiny. (54)

Joseph escaped to Egypt's land,
      being warned in a dream,
As Moses did in ancient sign
      when told so by the Bush.
He took the mother and the child,
      to fulfill Love's Song's verse,
"Out of Egypt I called my son,"
      this time for pride's disperse. (55)

When Herod died, the Child was safe,
      saw Joseph in a dream,
So he got up, through desert trod,
      and went to Nazareth,
The quiet town of their own birth,
      away from all the pace.
With family and his work around,
      it was a place of grace. (56)

Now Love's Song is a desert song,
    at times one strains to hear,
In barren hills of Galilee,
    the years are used to grow
In wisdom, stature, grace of God,
    and favor with all men,
For being framed in Mary's womb,
    His body's without sin. (57)

Year in, year out, this family kept
    the obligations due,
And Passover would have its feast
    up in Jerusalem.
The Love Song oft had sung of it,
    to sign salvation's ways,
Delivered by the Lamb of God,
    with blood the ransom pays. (58)

In those days an Hebrew boy,
    when judged to come of age,
Would blessing from his father take
    as Hebrew law prescribed.
Within that year of this Boy's life,
    the pilgrimage was made.
The last day they had left the place,
    unknown that Jesus stayed. (59)

One day out discovery's made
    in humble caravan,
That this Boy's not with Joseph's clan;
    in panic they return.
With three days search there's no resolve,
    for three days He's not seen.
Mary's heart can feel the pierce;
    she'll feel in future scene. (60)

They found him in the Temple courts,
    there singing Love's sweet song,
Amazing those who teach the law,
    with grasp of holy things.
When found, the anxious parents gasp,
    "Why did you treat us thus?"
"My Father's house is now My space;
    why did you make a fuss?" (61)

"Bar mitzvah" made, He then returned,
    and was obedient
To those His Father'd given Him
    to bring Him to His charge.
And so the boyhood of this One,
    in flesh, the living Word,
Was in a place of desert-ness,
    where Love's Song could be heard. (62)

In Hebrew ways, it's thirty years,
　　　　when one is said to be
Mature enough to counsel give
　　　　and take a teacher's place.
In desert land a man was found,
　　　　old Zechariah's son,
Sent there by God from barren womb,
　　　　precursor of the One. (63)

When he was born, his father said,
　　　　"God's prophet you will be,
For you will go before the Lord,
　　　　prepare the way for Him."
He now comes forth in desert sand,
　　　　to do what he's been told.
To make straight paths he must be brave
　　　　and be a preacher bold. (64)

"You brood of snakes, who cautioned you?
　　　　Prepare for wrath to come!
Show proof of penance made for sin,
　　　　on linage do not count.
The axe is now laid at the root,
　　　　of unproductive tree.
God can raise up Abraham's seed,
　　　　and by these stones decree." (65)

"What shall we do," the people asked,
  "how shall we know it's done?"
"With the poor share your clothes and food;
  the weak do not extort."
Love's Song's paradigm is preserved,
  for this has been Their theme.
To know God's love one must so love
  and give the poor esteem." (66)

It is Their way; it best gives one
  the proper view within,
For it is in that prospered heart,
  that Their love's oft denied.
So poverty becomes the field
  of interplay with God.
John, born to be the desert voice,
  knew well the Spirit's prod. (67)

John roamed the desert, heard the Wind,
  demanded purity.
As did Elijah in the past,
  he dressed in camel's hair.
With leather belt around his waist,
  he sang Love's poverty.
Wild honey, locusts were his feast;
  ascetic piety. (68)

He baptized with the ancient rite
     of cleansing and reform,
For Love's Song's tune would oft be played to
     aquatic's overture,
As from waters primordial,
     the Word brought ordered life.
Love saved that life in Noah's flood,
     while drowning out the strife. (69)

Love brought from Egypt, Israel's seed,
     and marched them through the sea,
And gave them desert's greatest need
     with water from the Rock,
Commanded cleansing of the priests
     who'd handle ritual course.
And when Love sang, it'd sound the same,
     like water's rushing force. (70)

A babe is formed in watered womb,
     and water precedes birth.
This ancient rite was done to sign
     the re-form of new life,
To cleanse and wash the sin away
     that clings in human hearts,
And lets one rise from bath of faith,
     to walk with a new start. (71)

In desert cults of John's own time,
     baptism was the sign
Of good intent to live the life
     of dedicated faith.
John so baptized with that in mind,
     With penance to inspire,
But preached another baptism
     of Spirit and of fire. (72)

"There's One among you even now,
     more powerful than I,
And He will winnow by his Hand,
     to break the chaff away,
To gather wheat into His barn,
     to clear the threshing floor."
Thus John spoke of the One to come,
     that Love Song's chant foreswore. (73)

Then Jesus came to Jordan's bank
     while John was baptizing,
And walked into the waters fresh,
     to be baptized by him.
"I have the need to come to You,
     and yet You come to me?"
"So let it be that we do this,
     for righteous destiny." (74)

What was this act that Son of God
     would need to be re-formed,
The Sinless One, birthed from above,
     who lives impeccably?
O Mystery, O Living God,
     what could this signify?
Was this bad taste, John in the right,
     to this request deny? (75)

Not for repentance this would be,
     but for a higher sign.
At age of judgment Jesus came,
     to demonstrate by Life,
To fully fill all of Love's Song,
     creating Way anew.
New covenant, new liturgy,
     new sacrifice that's true. (76)

John was birthed of the priestly tribe,
     old Zechariah's son,
But Jesus was of Judah born,
     to fulfill David's throne.
A new priesthood would be set forth,
     for all to expedite,
And now the High Priest of this set,
     is washed for solemn rite. (77)

'Twas David's psalm that sang Love's Song
      of future chair to fill,
With princely power from royal birth,
      to sit at God's right hand.
Of eternal King David sang,
      but also timeless Priest,
The order of Melchizedek,
      conferring on the least. (78)

Induction done by waters pure,
      the King-Priest then came up.
The heavens rent; the Dove was sent,
      anointing as the Seal.
Love then sang out, ordaining Him,
      as Father from above,
"This is my Son with whom I'm pleased,
      the One who is beloved." (79)

Love's Song is still a desert song
      and all who're sent to sing
Have by God's Breath been led out there,
      prepared by Voice of Love.
Now Voice Himself is sent by Wind,
      for fasting and for prayer,
To face the ancient tempter thrice,
      as in the garden fair. (80)

"Now if you are the Son of God,
          command bread from these stones.
For I know you are hungry now
          that you are flesh and bone."
The echo of Eve's deadly glare,
          enticed by appetite,
Rang in the conscience of this One,
          who'd come to mend the blight. (81)

"Man does not live by bread alone,
          'tis written in the scrolls,
But only by the Word that's sung
          by the sweet Voice of love."
For in the worldly order struck
          when time began by sin,
The lust of flesh has been a curse;
          desires have been an end. (82)

Then the devil took Him up
          to heights where He could see
All of the kingdoms of the world,
          o'er which this power ruled,
The very ones who Son would cleanse,
          the ones for whom He'd die.
The sin of want that pierced Eve's soul
          was imaged in His eye. (83)

"I will give you what you see,
        for that is my purview,
If you'd but for a moment bend
        the knee to me that's due."
"It is written, as you well know,
        to worship only God,
For He is Lord of all that is,
        He only shall one laud." (84)

No shortcut to Love's great desire
        to fell the wall of sin
That separates by fear and loss,
        creates a dearth within.
The lust of eyes that seeks the prize
        has been the deadly pit,
That those who dig, themselves fall in,
        the demon space unfit. (85)

Then next the devil had Him stand,
        on temple's parapet,
"If you are truly Son of God,
        throw yourself down from here.
For it is written, angels care,
        you'll stumble not, nor fall."
To tempt the Son for who He is
        was this vile serpent's call. (86)

Love's Song sang of a kingdom come,
     and Savior King to rule.
No one thought it would be the LORD,
     so how could they believe.
But if the Son just floated down
     from lofty temple perch,
All who would see would worship now,
     leave doubting in the lurch. (87)

Such was the devil's faulty thought,
     the thinking of gross pride,
To make a rift in unity,
     as Eden long ago
By pride of life in who one is,
     defending what is right,
By one's own will, in one's own way,
     on one's own strength delight. (88)

But, Jesus sang in simple tones,
     however sternly meant,
"You must not put the Lord your God
     to any proving test."
At that the devil finished this,
     by vanity he's tied
The three paths to the human heart:
     the eyes, the flesh, the pride. (89)

Love's Song is such a desert song,
      why was it sung so here?
For Son of Man, the Son of God,
      as such He cannot sin.
He gave the devil desert time,
      so to reverse the fall,
And show that Word is what is used
      to quell the tempter's gall. (90)

So Satan left Him at that time,
      'tis said in Holy Writ,
To wait the chance to try again,
      to thwart the Song of love.
He'll take the chance to find the fault
      in future field of play,
To find someone who'll see himself
      in prideful disarray. (91)

CANTO OF THE SONG OF LOVE

From the beginning, Love would sing
    combining Word and Breath.
Their timeless Love did enter time,
    make sacred history.
Voice would make known this Song of Love
    to those whose hearts would hear,
What patriarchs and prophets sang,
    the madrigal by ear. (1)

I AM now has a human sound,
    with passion resonant.
Voice made flesh will now sing the Song
    to woo the wayward heart,
Entwining grace and mercy set
    in strains of hidden things.
With Breath inflection is revealed
    what only Truth can sing. (2)

The introit's sung in Nazareth,
     the first to hear the claim,
Among those whom He grew and played,
     familiar faces all.
In synagogue Isaiah's scroll,
     was handed Him to read.
He found the place of Love's Song's theme,
     the stating of His creed. (3)

"The Spirit of the Lord's on Me,
     to preach unto the poor,
To proclaim freedom to the bound,
     and sight to all the blind,
Relieve oppressed, announce the year
     of favor of the Lord.
Today what's said in sacred writ.
     is fulfilled in this chord." (4)

Now, Love's Song is a desert song,
     and renders lyrics such,
The desert of the poor and bound,
     the blind and the oppressed
Will be the aim of Song and Dance,
     where Song's reception's done,
And it remains the only space,
     where hearts can hear Love spun. (5)

Familiar-ness oft breeds contempt,
    the adage seems to go.
"How can this be, for we know him,
    isn't he Joseph's son?"
It is the truth without a doubt,
    a prophet's honor giv'n,
'Cept in his town, by his own kin,
    and out of town He's driv'n. (6)

Along the sea he called some men,
    to come and follow Him.
They dropped their nets when their hearts throbbed,
    responding to the song.
Another left his tax accounts;
    soon twelve had been retained
To teach them this cantata's score,
    so they'd sing Love's refrain. (7)

He led them to the desert fields
    of poverty and sin,
And dealt with pride that wills its way,
    especially in them.
It is the meek who's view of self
    can see to rise above,
And they're the ones who in their heart
    now hear the Heart of Love. (8)

He showed them how pride from the start
      fell prey to Satan's lie,
And how vainglory wormed its way
      into religious life.
He taught them all how fear of faith
      is oft love's enemy,
And sang to them the choruses
      where Love's the guarantee. (9)

He worked the works of miracles,
      as signs of Who He Is,
That sickness and disease are oft
      the prodigy of fear.
That blindness of the human eyes
      is cause for Mercy's touch:
That blindness of the human heart
      is more the deadly clutch. (10)

He showed His pow'r o'er all that is
      with might and sovereignty.
He calmed the sea, restored lame limbs,
      and made the demons flee.
He fed the crowds, cleansed leprosy;
      He raised the dead to life.
He blessed the children, forgave sin,
      brought peace amid the strife. (11)

For Love's Song is a desert song
     where selflessness can hear,
Beyond the acts of care or need,
     the Lover's true intent.
What pride cannot, love can see
     and feel the desert Wind,
And come to know within the heart
     the meaning deep within. (12)

He sang as none had sung before,
     of precepts in the heart.
Beneath the murder as the sin,
     'twas anger at the root.
Instead of letting sexual sin
     destroy the bond of two,
Quell selfish lust that's in the heart,
     for that's where true hope's due. (13)

Of love He had the most to say,
     like "love your enemies."
Forgiveness frees the path for love
     restoring man or God,
And "love the Lord with all your heart,
     your soul, strength, and mind.
And love your neighbor as yourself"
     …that's all of it combined. (14)

He gave one command to his band,
     to sing to those who'll hear,
"Love one another with My love,"
     all else will fall in place.
For Love's Song's theme is love itself,
     the heart of God doth flow.
To that extent He said He'd show
     how far that Love will go. (15)

He taught them of a kingdom come,
     a place of holiness,
At once uniting all that's True,
     of what is There brought here.
He let them know how it would be
     when in God's realm they'd walk,
And how so few would follow them,
     at faith and love would balk. (16)

Yeast would invade, the yeast of pride,
     the leaven of old ways,.
Unleavened bread of purity
     should be the manna stored.
That it would be a treasure sought,
     when found, a treasure bought.
The price He'd pay would be for all
     the field where treasure's caught. (17)

He took three men aside one day,
      revealing mystery,
Convened with Moses of the law,
      with prophet Elijah,
To show that what was sung before
      in Him would be fulfilled,
For "He's my Son, the One I love,"
      in Him the Song's instilled. (18)

Instead of law, grace would abound,
      and prophecies be filled.
Righteousness, peace, and joy will kiss
      within the human heart,
And mystery that once was hid
      in ages of the past,
Would be made known to all the world,
      in Him the dye was cast. (19)

THE CANTO OF THE DANCE

Within three years He laid the course,
    which caused the rise and fall,
As Simeon had so foretold,
    the joust of truth and pride.
Those who adorned with vanity,
    their hearts filled with conceit,
Fell into rage against the love
    that threatened Moses' seat. (1)

Hypocrites, blind guides they were,
    their minds bound by the rules,
So much so that when God passed by,
    they recognized Him not.
When one no longer hears the Song,
    for striving with the score,
Idol's made of ability,
    displacing passion's store. (2)

"I am the Way of Truth and Life,"
     He'd sing the descant pure,
So pure it caused discordant tone
     with what the teachers taught.
And then sang He veraciously,
     in universal sync,
"I AM...I AM" before what was,
     with God He made the link. (3)

From that time on, they sought His death,
     in Lucifer-on style,
As in the time before time was,
     when plotting caused the fall.
The people though, could hear the Song,
     for they in desert roamed.
The plotters could not get to Him for
     fear they'd be disowned. (4)

So waited they to seize the day
     when they could still the Voice,
But little did they know the Song,
     nor what the words implied.
That all be done as prophesied
     and all the signs fulfilled;
That Love's Song sang from before time,
     all of eternal Will. (5)

Foremost among the signs of yore
      would be the exodus,
That's celebrated year by year
      in Feast of Passover.
A lamb was slain; the blood was brushed
      with hyssop's bushy bough,
A meal of lamb, unleavened bread,
      and wine to seal the vow. (6)

The King came to Jerusalem,
      creating quite a stir,
He rode an ass to show intent
      to be the Prince of peace.
The people hailed Him on the road,
      palm branches they all waved,
The symbol of good harvest yield,
      Messiah's come to save. (7)

Love's Song will now crescendo build,
      for in the temple courts,
The children's choir sings Song aloud,
      disturbing pious prayers.
"Make them desist this senseless laud!"
      the priest and scribes rang out,
"Have you not read the child will praise?"
      He said amid the rout. (8)

The children's heart has pure intent,
    unlearned of prideful ways.
Their simple heart's a desert where
    the Wind is free to blow.
Love thus belongs to such as these,
    and if you're not like that,
Love's Song you cannot clearly hear;
    the tone of It is flat. (9)

The music's modulation shifts;
    the lyrics grow intense.
A movement of suspense is heard;
    the dance begins to stir.
The Son sings oft of suffering,
    of life beyond the veil.
Anointed with the balm of love,
    He sings of burial. (10)

The Feast of Passover draws nigh,
    the feast that must be kept,
The feast that Son will meaning give
    for all eternity.
He gathers in an upper room,
    as in the bondage days,
With twelve to keep the Seder meal,
    deliverance to praise. (11)

Before they ate, He knew His hour
　　　of love was soon to come.
To show His love to those He chose,
　　　He signed the full extent.
With water basin in His hands
　　　and girded with a towel,
He knelt before each one of them,
　　　as only servant shall. (12)

He washed their feet, so clean they'd be
　　　for this was Holy Ground,.
"Not me, no, never mine you'll wash,"
　　　said Peter, feet withdrawn.
He thought he'd spoken in belief
　　　as faithful devotee,
But sometimes faith can host a pride
　　　that keeps the song off key. (13)

Said Jesus in reply to him
　　　who'd lead them all some day,
"Forbid Me not to wash your feet,
　　　or have no part with Me."
"Not just my feet, but hands and head'"
　　　said Peter in reply.
When faith is jarred, it often on
　　　the opposite relies. (14)

"A person bathed needs only wash
    away the daily dirt.
And clean you are, except for one,"
    sang Jesus for he knew
Who it would be the tempter would
    be able to entice,
Who by his pride would betray Him,
    whose purse would hold the price. (15)

They all fell prey to sadness now,
    each looked at their own pride,
And stated in half-hearted tone,
    "Oh, surely, Lord, not I."
If one believes he cannot do
    the one thing he abhors,
He is open to Satan's lies,
    sin's lurking at the door. (16)

When meal was set, He said to them,
    "I have desired to eat,"
For Love had set this ancient meal,
    and Love fulfills it now.
He took the bread, gave thanks for it,
    and gave it to them all,
"This is My Body given up,
    to eat as you recall." (17)

Then after meal, before the hymn,
 He took the cup of wine,
The third cup of this sacred meal,
 He took within His hands,
"This is my blood, poured out for you,
 in covenant that's new,"
Of sins forgiven, life made new,
 the sacrifice imbue. (18)

Of late they'd heard Him speak of this,
 but understood it not,
Of giving of His flesh to eat,
 and drinking of His blood,
Eternal Life to life be giv'n
 in Love's most selfless act,
His flesh without Adamic blight,
 His blood in holy pact. (19)

"This is My Flesh," He said, "My Blood,
 and it is true indeed,
That whosoever eats this Meal,
 in Me remains always:
My flesh, the food, My Blood, the drink
 of what I will to do.
I'll sacrifice My Life for all,
 that Life may be in you." (20)

They took the Cup in wonderment,
     for He sang a new Song.
Each drank from It, not sure of It,
     but sure that it was True.
Suddenly, after psalmic chant,
     He rose from table fare,
And went out to a garden near
     without the closing prayer. (21)

Judas, in darkness, left the group
     in haste to do the deed.
He made the deal he surely thought
     would fix Messiah's cause,
To rid fair Israel of Rome,
     by striking Caesar's hand.
How proud he was, to be a part
     of God's redemptive plan. (22)

How wrong he was, how dreadful wrong,
     to think he'd know at all,
For Love's ways are unsearchable,
     Love's paths cannot be traced,
But sight is blinded by one's pride
     and will not wait for light.
Since Adam's time God's purposes
     are lost in such a night. (23)

The Son would sing while on the way,
     preparing hearts aflame,
"This is the night that most of you
     will also fall away."
"Not so," said Peter once again,
     so proud to show his all,
"They might so fall because of You,
     but I will not withdraw." (24)

Love's Song is still a desert song,
     and oft the singing's blurred
By pride that drifts the sands of soul,
     and makes the traveler blind.
"On this night, on this very night,
     your words will prove just show,
For three times you'll deny My call,
     before the rooster crows." (25)

"But, even if I die with You,
     I know You are the One!"
And one and all said just the same,
     denying desert soul.
'Tis hard to walk by faith, not sight,
     admit one's emptiness,
And wait for God to show the way,
     or fill the heart's abyss. (26)

He entered dark Gethsemane,
     and took three deeper in,
Then going farther than they all,
     looked up and prayed to Love,
That Glory would be His He had
     before the world was framed.
He prayed for these who followed Him,
     and those He's yet to claim. (27)

He knew of divine destiny,
     and that He faced the cross.
Not wavering from sacred course,
     He prayed most earnestly,
The cup of shame that'd blaspheme Love,
     would not be what's at stake,
That blasphemy would play a role,
     and that He could not take. (28)

The scourging and the cross of death,
     He'd gladly bear for all,
But hearing Their Love vilified,
     caused anxious drops of blood.
For love can take its own attacks,
     and stand up to the scorn,
But when the loved is brought a charge,
     the lover's heart is torn. (29)

Three times He asked this cup to pass,
    in total agony.
Three times He's met with silence dark,
    and thrice request denied.
So He must dance the Dance of Love,
    and take the bane of pride,
To abrogate the curse of sin
    where Love cannot abide. (30)

He rose from there to face the Dance
    that's driven by the love
That has so often thrust itself
    upon the stage of time,
But now's the moment of its part;
    it's no rehearsal here,
Now is all history summed up,
    man's meaning made most clear. (31)

They came with torches, swords, and clubs,
    as if He was a knave.
This crowd sent from those liable
    for keeping Moses' seat.
No pride exceeds religious pride,
    where orthodoxy's kept.
No fear deeper will then strike out,
    accused of false concept. (32)

In the darkness they would be sure
    to seize the Holy One.
Dark Judas had arranged the scene,
    choreographed with care.
There he was in front of them all,
    the one who would betray
With but a kiss of love intent
    on having its own way. (33)

If Son's arrest were then and there,
    and taken to the court,
He'll have to prove He's Who He Is
    with power that's divine.
Launch freedom's march against Rome's grip,
    which is Messiah's cue,
And zealots will free Israel,
    God's Kingdom will come through. (34)

Thus Judas had it figured out,
    the same as Eden's lapse.
Such pride will often cause a course
    where Love cannot abide.
Thus was the reason for the kiss
    that marked rebellion's thrill,
To press upon the sands of time
    pride's presumptuous will. (35)

Confronting Him with knives and clubs,
     He knew of their intent,
And sensing pride's defensive stroke
     in those who were His own.
"Who is it that you want?" He asked.
     "Jesus the Nazarene."
"I AM," the One as from the Bush,
     the One who was unseen. (36)

At that, they fell away enmasse
     as if that were enough,
But pride makes reason impotent,
     so they came back again.
"I told you I'm the One," Son sang,
     this time in muted tone,
"Let these men go; its Me you want,
     It's Me and Me alone." (37)

But, Peter who in pride had pledged,
     defending honor due,
Then drew a sword, struck in the dark,
     cut off a servant's ear.
When pride reacts defensively
     and blind to Love's revere,
It strikes amiss discordant notes,
     that none can bear to hear. (38)

So Son replaced the severed ear,
        rebuking Peter's strike.
The sword of pride will lead to death,
        but meekness drinks the cup.
They took the Son to temple's court,
        to face the charges stacked.
Exaggerated lies were said;
        the testimony hacked. (39)

Outside the court a fire was kept,
        to warm the temple guards,
A servant girl who, passing by,
        remembered Peter's face,
"You're also with the Nazarene
        and you are one of them."
"I don't know what you're saying, girl:"
        he feared he'd be condemned. (40)

She said again to those around,
        "This one is one of them."
Again denial from the one
        who said he'd never fail.
The third time she was sure of it,
        she'd heard his accent plain,
To which he cursed and swore to them,
        to show her statement vain. (41)

At once he heard the rooster crow,
      and his Lord turned and looked.
The memory came bursting in;
      his character collapsed.
In shame he went out to the dark,
      and there wept bitter tears,
For Love had sung to him that night,
      revealing pride that fears. (42)

The daybreak came and with it was
      determination bound
To rid their world of this fraud bold,
      who called Himself the One.
"Are you the Christ?" they questioned Him,
      "It's you who say I AM."
The high priest rent his garments then,
      "He blasphemes in this sham." (43)

When Judas heard they had condemned
      the Holy One of God,
And he'd not seen the Son give proof,
      as when the storm He stilled,
He came to those he used to scheme
      and sing delusion's score.
He threw the price of his pride's bluff
      upon the temple floor. (44)

When sin commits against one loved,
    acknowledging what's true,
Often the pride does not forgive,
    condemning lover's heart.
Conviction ought to be what's known,
    to clear the way for grace.
But pride will condemnation bring,
    adjudicating case. (45)

So Judas went and hanged himself,
    the prosecutor played,
And also took the seat of judge,
    'tis pride's conceited role.
They led Son off to Pilate's house,
    the man who Rome enclaved,
For death was not in their purview,
    and death is what they craved. (46)

"He claims to be the Christ," they said,
    "and claims king of the Jews.
He stirs the people up with words,
    not teaching as we do."
"This is no matter worth my time,
    put Him in Herod's court."
This Herod was the lustful king
    who made the Baptist sport. (47)

Herod thus was greatly pleased,
    for he had heard of Him,
And hoped to see a magic show,
    instead of Love's Song's words.
So Jesus would not sing a word,
    though plied with questions' probe,
Then Herod taunted Jesus' claim,
    and gave Him kingly robe. (48)

To Pilate's house again He's sent,
    the Dance of Love begins.
"I find no evidence of wrong;
    I find no fault in Him.
I'll scourge Him and release Him then,"
    was Pilate's judgment staid.
"I've found no cause for Him to die,
    nor of incitement made." (49)

"Away with Him, away with Him!"
    the priests and scribes all cried.
"Release to us Barabbas bold,
    for insurrection held."
Just Pilate tried to mediate,
    but they all turned deaf ear.
"Crucify Him! Crucify Him!"
    they shouted in their fear. (50)

For fear it is that feeds the heart,
     when truth exposes pride,
Not hate nor evil intent coined,
     but fear of lost control.
"What has He done to deserve death?"
     was Pilate's swift retort.
But they cried out insistently,
     injustice to extort. (51)

The Roman could not understand
     and failed to quit the charge.
He washed his hands of this cruel jest,
     the sign of innocence.
"Then let His blood be on our heads,"
     the mob was quick to say,
Yes, His blood be on their heads,
     on this atonement day. (52)

So off He went, this Son of God,
     to dance the Dance of Love.
Tied to the flogging post secure,
     bared to the flagellum,
Skin shredded there, his back in stripes,
     the Blood will trickle down.
Love bought for us these stripes that cure
     where sickness would be found. (53)

The soldiers mocked this King of kings,
    dressed Him in Herod's robe.
They made a helmet-crown for Him
    and pierced His head with thorns.
His scepter was a twig in hand;
    His praise was their disdain.
They knelt to Him, they spit on Him,
    they struck Him time again. (54)

Then when they thought Him weak enough,
    they went to get the cross,
Unfinished cross-beam used before,
    tied on His arms spread wide.
So when He fell, as sure He would,
    His face received the blow.
He struggled out into the way,
    the whole scene one of woe. (55)

Their plans and dreams were now condemned;
    the women mourned and wailed.
"Weep not for Me, but for your own,"
    He gasped to them in pain.
He was too weak; He fell too much,
    the soldiers would not wait,
So they pressed a Cyrenean
    to carry that gross weight. (56)

His mother's somewhere in the crowd;
      her heart is pierced by this.
For surely she is reeling, too,
      by watching such a Dance.
But, surely too, what has come forth
      from deep within her heart,
Are all the moments pondered there,
      and knowing from the start. (57)

The hill is reached; the stipes are there,
      the posts for crosses crude.
The guard offered some wine to drink;
      with gall it dulled the pain.
But He refused; He'd bear the pain
      and suffering for sure.
They stripped Him then, the greatest shame
      a Hebrew could endure. (58)

He took the nails in hands of flesh,
      and thus He proved His kin.
When love is hurt, the loved is hurt
      and bears the pain as well.
They hung the cross upon the stipe
      and used His feet to brace.
Then casting lots for bloody clothes,
      they kept watch o'er the place. (59)

The crucified is within reach
      for people to rebuff.
The whole affair is hardly o'er
      a person's standard height.
They spit; they cursed; they pulled His beard,
      'twas part of such a game,
So pride insulted Son that day
      and blasphemed Holy Name. (60)

The cup of wrath from those He loved,
      the cup He prayed would pass,
He drank that day, drank to the full,
      that Love they would recall,
That They who in that love made man,
      would show the full extent,
Of when They made the image pure,
      They'd now show Their intent. (61)

Love so intense, sweet Mystery,
      amid such bitterness.
Fear so replete from pride's conceit,
      they railed on Son's Love Dance.
"Forgive them, Father," He absolved,
      "They know not what they do."
This mob caught up in pride's conspire
      will never face this rue. (62)

"You'll build the temple in three days,
      but cannot save yourself!
Come down from there, and we'll believe,"
      the mockers ridiculed.
Two thieves where also put to death;
      one joined the crowd's disgust,
"If you are the messiah king,
      so save yourself and us." (63)

"Don't you fear God?" the other snapped,
      "We get what we have earned..
In your kingdom remember me."
      he said in his reserve.
"Today, indeed you'll be with Me,"
      the Son said from the wood.
"Today you'll be in paradise,"
      Love's Dance is understood. (64)

For Love's Song is a desert song,
      and heard with desert heart,
That won't deny aridity,
      but see through desert eyes.
That Love accepts confessions made
      while facing death's cold stare,
Preempts the sacraments of grace,
      that Adam's race must share. (65)

The Son then looked in front of Him,
    and saw His mother there,
And standing loyally at her side,
    the one who Jesus loved.
Jesus was Mary's only born,
    her care His lawful due,
For Moses said the firstborn son
    was obligated true. (66)

Without another to release
    his mother's precious life,
He looks at her through blood-stained eyes,
    "Woman, here is your son."
And saying to the one he loved,
    "Here is your mother, now."
Thus true to her in death's release,
    completes the moral vow. (67)

Soon darkness came upon the land,
    the sun refused to shine.
Impaled upon the bitter tree
    was Word who made that star.
How can this be that these He made,
    could do this to the Word?
"They need my light so they might live,
    so my light I've deferred." (68)

Son hung suspended for three hours
     while sun refused to shine.
"My God, My God" He cried aloud,
     "Why do You forsake Me?"
What is this cry that thinks that Love
     can ere forsake the Son?
Love's not forsaken, not ignored;
     it never has been done! (69)

In Him was Life, the Light of men;
     no darkness can o'ertake,
But sign of such the sun enacts,
     and Love had not rebuked.
How can this Life, Eternal Life,
     be o'ercome by this death,
But that the Father of all flesh
     allow this breach of Breath? (70)

As in the water's pious sign,
     no breathing's in the plunge,
So it will be that on this tree,
     that sinless flesh must die.
The time has come, the time of times,
     that takes all of sin's pain.
The Son of Love, the Word made flesh,
     becomes the Lamb that's slain. (71)

But could the Son be so denied,
        could Trinity take death?
Son's greatest pleasure's always been
        obeying Father's Will,
And though He's equal in all things,
        as always He'll comply,
And nothing He'll make of Himself,
        but Father's Love rely. (72)

For Love's Song is a desert song,
        and Lamb of God a sign
Who stands before the shearers dumb,
        in sacrificial Love.
It's pride that fills the human heart,
        and blinds one to God's Will,
But agony is questioned here,
        and waits for God to still. (73)

Could He have saved Himself that day?
        As God, could He come down?
No! Rings the answer loud and clear,
        for God cannot transgress.
To disobey would be the sin
        that'd blemish Lamb of God.
No longer He would Holy be
        ...the Savior would be flawed. (74)

The Paschal Lamb is ready now;
 the Son is knowing this,
That all things are accomplished now,
 completed to the end.
Knowing that all was now in place,
 and knowing from the first,
Amid the noise of pride's burlesque,
 He simply said, "I thirst." (75)

The desert Dance must be complete
 to consecrate the feast.
The Seder supper's final cup
 had not been drunk that night.
The hymn was sung, but Jesus went
 to start His passion rite,
The fourth and final cup was left
 for revelation's light. (76)

A jar of sour wine was there;
 they soaked it with a sponge,
Stuck that upon a hyssop branch,
 from which He quenched His thirst.
The meal's complete, all signs fulfilled,
 which signaled for the end.
The meal will now transition make,
 to holiness ascend. (77)

"This is My Body, this My Blood,"
    and soon it would make sense,
"Eat and drink and remain in Me
    …let Me remain in you."
As blood with hyssop branch was smeared
    upon the bondage doors,
So now death passes over all,
    who with this Blood are scored. (78)

The Passover presider's word,
    as custom would dictate,
At supper's end, with confidence,
    he should intone the words,
"It is finished," for one and all
    to know the rite is done.
So Son addresses one and all,
    "It's Finished"…Love has won. (79)

Then Voice gives all to Father's Will,
    He cries for all to hear,
"Into Your Hands, My Spirit place,"
    He bowed His head and died.
The Word made flesh departs the stage.
    The Song of Love seemed done.
The Dance was o'er, the music waned,
    and angels all were stunned. (80)

The rocks were rent, the graves erupt,
      the temple curtain split,
The earth rebels and death's confused,
      at heaven's access made.
This must be the end of time
      for He who Is, seemed not,
But Love soon stilled the growing tide,
      for they knew not Love's plot. (81)

Passover's special Sabbath's near;
      this day they must prepare,
No bodies can be on the cross;
      no hands must touch the dead.
Pilate permits that legs be broke,
      so death can overtake.
The lungs will fill with fluid then;
      the victims suffocate. (82)

They broke the legs of nearby thief,
      the other, did the same.
Then found the Son already dead;
      they did not break His legs.
Such Mystery, such profound deed,
      the Son had made the call.
Divinity they could not kill,
      so Love had given all. (83)

He was not killed upon a cross,
        nor executed there.
He was no victim of the court,
        not Hebrew nor of Rome.
'Twas sung so clear at Seder meal,
        "My Body giv'n for you."
He's in control of Mystery;
        the cross is but the cue. (84)

The Passover Lamb is now slain,
        but no bone must be broke.
The spotless Lamb will yield its life,
        to celebrate the night
That signed the breaking of the yoke,
        escape from death's cold brink.
Unleavened bread would be the sop,
        and wine the rightful drink. (85)

"This is my Body, giv'n for you"
        He had set the score,
Then sang the Song and danced the Dance,
        fulfilling passion's plan.
"There is no greater love than this,"
        He was want to say,
"Than one lay down his life for friends,"
        and that became the Way. (86)

He was no victim of their pride,
      no dupe upon the cross.
'Twas Adam's sin that put Him there,
      if victim is the word.
Love wrote this opera for the Son,
      and Breath bred Mary's womb.
Before foundation of the world,
      the Lamb slain was assumed. (87)

When guard found Son hanging so still,
      surprised, he must have proof.
With lance he pierced the Sacred Heart,
      and Blood and Water flowed,
To show that death had truly set,
      and pride's mean prize was lost.
The Blood is shed; the Water poured:
      Sacrament's sublime cost. (88)

Passover now has been fulfilled,
      the Blood is on the wood.
The price is paid: the Lamb of God
      who takes away all sin.
The sacrifice will be recalled
      through ages yet to come,
By water, word, and sacred meal,
      and living in the Son. (89)

A member of Sanhedrin's rank,
     by Joseph he was called,
Required the Body of the Son
     and took it from the cross.
Was Mary there? Did she receive
     the Body to caress?
Did she help wash and swaddle it,
     as in the birthing stress? (90)

What scenes replayed in her pure heart
     as she looked in His Face?
Was in her heart sustaining grace
     because she knew the truth?
The Sabbath day begins at eve;
     she must inter the Word
In unused tomb, as in her womb,
     the virgin's faith deferred. (91)

The tomb was quickly filled that day,
     a stone rolled in its door.
'Twas borrowed, unbeknown to them,
     for just the next three days.
Love borrowed grotto for His birth,
     and manger, too, the same.
The ass He rode, the upper room,
     and, too, the cross of shame. (92)

But Voice no longer was incased
      in this dead fleshly shrine,
But in the unseen world of death
      Love's Song was being sung.
Hades was sore distressed that day,
      for Life walked in its midst,
And death, the wage of prideful life,
      no longer is a mist. (93)

The Son had entered Sheol's realm,
      to take away its sting,
That those who in its chorus sing,
      will not be in its pow'r.
From this day on, instead of dread,
      'tis death that sets one free,
And is the rite of passage for
      the life of victory. (94)

To die to sin and die to self,
      through faith and penance borne,
And be baptized into His death,
      as crucified with Son.
It is no longer prideful doom,
      but Life of Christ to yield.
Then corporal death no longer holds,
      but ceaseless life reveals. (95)

They laid His Body in a tomb,
     a place to rest in peace,
But unbeknown to them He's not
     confined to such a bed.
Nor is He waiting for Love's pow'r
     to burst forth from the grave.
He's singing of the pow'r instead,
     that's in the Blood He gave. (96)

He gave Himself to this cold realm,
     that knows no rich or poor,
Where young or old are not exempt
     from death's consuming grip.
From garden's fall the flesh of man
     has faced this unknown cage
Where good and bad, where right and wrong
     have reaped transgressions wage. (97)

But on that day amidst eclipse
     and quaking of the earth,
One came into this chamber bare,
     this desert dark and dry,
Who did not enter taken down,
     but came by His own dare.
He'd given Self to deal with death,
     and end this dreaded snare. (98)

He marched right through the gates of death,
 which only open in,
And with the Voice that freedom brings,
 brought light into the dark.
By that same Word that those had heard
 in desert hearts of pride,
He set the captives free that day
 from being cast aside. (99)

And then this Victor turned around
 and marched right out again,
Through those same gates He exit made,
 where only entrance was.
Sheol's gates no longer hold
 those put into its grasp.
Death has no sting, no victory,
 has no eternal clasp. (100)

Son, by the Word that had been flesh,
 allowed death's shroud to touch,
But, when He did cold death was changed,
 transformed from fear to faith.
What was the tyrant of distress,
 the overlord of strife,
The unknown specter held in awe,
 became the bark of life. (101)

Death, who had changed the rich to poor,
    now turned the poor to rich.
By grace the Voice of majesty
    submitted to the cross,
That for the sake of humankind
    death would be swallowed up
And become the friend of all
    who drink from Love Song's cup. (102)

For Love Song is a desert song,
    and death a desert made,
But on that day, death's desert sand
    became the stream to life.
A peaceful stream to those who yield
    their will to Son's true Way,
A course to take one through the veil
    to Everlasting Day. (103)

Again, 'tis water that's the sign
    where death is entered in,
And water that's the tomb of death
    where bondage is set free
By Blood that's shed in death's cold clutch,
    and water has been signed,
By Breath that breathes with life re-birthed,
    redemption is enshrined. (104)

The one who'd fallen from the Light,
        who brought death down to earth,
Thought he had stilled Love's Song's recite
        by using pride to kill.
What next took place in timelessness,
        that brought angelic gasp,
Forever sealed the liar's pow'r,
        and conquered that cruel asp. (105)

Sometime in early morning hours,
        the first day of the week,
When sun was made to shine again,
        the darkness to retrieve,
The earth, this time at Love's command,
        reacted in a quake.
An angel, bright as bright can be,
        rolled back the stone to wait. (106)

The angels were amazed, were awed;
        they'd not seen this before.
When Son received the Judas kiss,
        the angels yearned to aid,
No doubt were stunned when Son was flogged,
        one glance all it would take,
Or on the way to Calvary,
        or when nailed to the stake. (107)

But, Love forbade and held them back,
     the legions were restrained,
For they knew not the movements yet...
     the dance of desert song.
So when confounded they observed,
     that Love's Dance was not o'er,
That He'd be raised to sing and dance
     a supernal encore. (108)

Son, it seems, had just walked away
     amid dawn's complex hue,
With no eyewitness of the sight
     upon which all depends.
For if the Son has not been raised,
     then all He said and did
Goes unconfirmed with all He claimed;
     the Mystery stays hid. (109)

But, Love's Song is a desert song,
     the mind must be laid bare,
For this event must be content
     to rest on faith alone.
What no eye sees, what no ear hears,
     what no heart has conceived,
Becomes the source of greatest need,
     eternal life achieved. (110)

When there's no witness to the fact,
    then evidence must rule,
And faith alone becomes the trust
    upon which truth doth rest.
An empty tomb, a shroud laid neat,
    a silence that is rife,
Becomes the desert place to know
    that Love has given Life. (111)

That Rome had stationed guards around,
    was the High Priest's request,
And they were frozen in sheer fright,
    confusion's final state.
Some women came with spices sweet,
    the unction death appoints,
But found the stone had rolled away,
    no body to anoint. (112)

They saw the angel sitting there,
    not one but two of them,
"Why look for Life among the dead?
    He's not here; He's risen.
Remember now that He once said,
    He'd be refused by men,
Be crucified, and in three days,
    He would be raised again." (113)

The women hasten from that place
     to where disciples hid,
"It's as He said that it would be;
     He has been raised again!"
John outran Peter to the tomb,
     to see what it would show,
But Peter pushed past John to look,
     believed, and came to know. (114)

Deserted tomb becomes the place
     of evidence laid bare,
And hearts that have been broke of pride
     will see through eyes of faith.
He saw just linens lying there
     in death's cold chamber laid,
And they, the sign of all that's left
     of fleshly journey made. (115)

For those who enter such a space
     by putting pride away,
Will know that what is to be left
     in shedding self's conceit
Must then be folded purposely,
     an act of heart atoned,
And left in crucifixion's tomb,
     forever un-condoned. (116)

Returning to the upper room,
      not knowing what to do,
Peter slumped down in dismal pain,
      in condemnation's pit.
He had abandoned and denied,
      and now its proven true,
O damn this pride, this fear of love,
      now death should be what's due. (117)

The Magdalene had stayed thereby,
      to mourn in desert den,
Looked in the tomb and as she wept
      she saw the two in white,
"Why are you crying?" She replied,
      "They've taken Him away."
When love has lost, the desert creeps,
      and hope becomes its prey. (118)

And seeing someone standing there,
      she bravely asked of him,
"If you have taken Him away,
      His body I'll retrieve."
"Mary," He spoke to desert heart
      …He simply said her name,
But Voice is known by those in love,
      and Love's Song makes its claim. (119)

"Do not hold on to Me," He said,
     for she had lingered there.
The tomb's no place for love like this,
     for it must be fulfilled.
Return to glory, He had prayed,
     to glory as before,
The One Who's raised must so ascend
     to throne forevermore. (120)

If love's to be the sacrament
     that bonds all in the Three,
Then love desires the most it is,
     its fullness to receive.
In Him's the Fullness, All in all,
     the width, the depth, the height,
That those so loved may be complete,
     for so 'tis Love's requite. (121)

"Go tell my brothers what you've heard,"
     the Magdalene was told.
"I must return to Father now,
     to My God, and to yours."
Then Mary hastened with the news,
     and told them of His role.
They thought her in distress, they knew
     that she had loved Him so. (122)

The afternoon of that same day,
      two men dejected walked
Back to their home, disconsolate,
      for they had lost their hope.
Unknown to them, the Son came by
      and joined them on the way.
They were surprised He had not heard
      of horror's great display. (123)

They told Him of the Nazarene,
      of what they thought of Him,
Of how He died, and what it meant,
      as far as they could know.
That now some women bore the news,
      from tomb in which He lay
That angels said He was alive,
      the tomb an empty bay. (124)

"We thought for sure He was the One,
      redeeming Israel.
But now, alas, our hope is dashed,
      for these events are true."
"How foolish," the Sojourner said,
      "how slow of heart you be.
The Christ must suffer all these things,
      then enter His glory." (125)

Then starting there He sang Love's Song,
      so opening their hearts,
The Moses days, what prophets saw,
      He sang Love's Song to them.
For Love's Song is a desert song
      and only desert plays
The role of openness to Love
      gives meaning in the haze. (126)

At journey's end, they reached their place,
      He mentioned going on,
But they urged Him to stay with them
      because it was so late.
At suppertime He took the bread,
      gave thanks, and broke it there.
The myst'ry fell; they knew Him then,
      no longer faith impaired. (127)

In memory He's most assured
      in simple bread and wine.
"This is my Body, this my Blood,"
      real presence He will claim.
When in Love's feast He gives Himself,
      to celebrate the Cross,
He will assure encounter there,
      with love each heart emboss. (128)

Soon He'll tell his brothers, too,
    and they must sojourn join,
And open desert heart's distress
    by preaching of the Son,
For He indeed will go beyond,
    to heaven's Throne above.
Yet, in the breaking of the Bread,
    He'll be the source of Love. (129)

That ev'ning in the upper room
    where fear was hiding out,
Love penetrated the locked door
    and entered desert gloom.
"Peace be with you," the greeting came,
    He showed them hands and side.
It's perfect love that drives out fear
    and heals the wounds of pride. (130)

"Just as the Father has sent Me,
    so I will now send you."
With that He breathed God's Holy Breath
    upon each one of them.
"Who you forgive will be set free,
    and who you don't will not."
For when this Love breaks through closed doors,
    forgiveness must be wrought. (131)

Now Thomas was not in the room
    and missed this joyful scene.
When he did come, they sang to him,
    "We all have seen the One!"
"I'll not believe," was the retort,
    "I know that He is dead.
Unless I see and feel His wounds
    I'll keep this hopeless dread." (132)

A week goes by in cloistered fear;
    Thomas was there this time.
The brothers were still gathered hid,
    for want of what to do.
The Son came in and greeted them,
    "Shalom, peace be with you."
Then just for Thomas Love supplied
    the proof for him to view. (133)

No finger in the wounded hands,
    no hand thrust in the side.
The beatific sight o'ercame
    dry desert's unbelief.
And Thomas was the first to claim
    what angels sing about,
"My Lord!" he cried in sure belief,
    "My God!" beyond all doubt! (134)

It's oft the case when desert hearts
  are injured in events,
Break through their fear to hear Love's Song,
  become the most convinced.
The deeper goes the wounds of pride,
  the deeper Love doth heal,
But Love's Song penetrates the core,
  rejection to repeal. (135)

Peter still felt the bitter shame
  of selfishness and pride.
He was not worthy of the band
  who felt such faith and love.
He went to fish in Galilee
  and muse upon his ache;
Nathanael, Thomas, James and John
  went with him for his sake. (136)

They fished at night, for that's what's done;
  the fish avoid the sun.
At night the nets are cast about,
  for fish on surface feed.
In early morning's fog there stood
  a stranger on the shore,
"Friends," He called out, "caught anything?"
  They knew not Love's Song's score. (137)

"No," they called out from desert's boat,
     "Nothing is in our nets."
When fishing's done unsure of Love,
     the net will empty be.
"So throw your nets on the right side,"
     the stranger said to shift,
And doing so, they took a haul
     impossible to lift. (138)

The Voice that's known by love-filled heart
     was known by youngest there.
He told Peter for he was sure,
     "It is the Lord!" John said.
And Peter clothed his nakedness;
     he felt the pain break in,
As in primeval garden's shame,
     he sought to cover sin. (139)

As in the desert, so 'tis here,
     there is no place to hide,
So Peter jumped into the lake,
     let water cover pride.
The boat came next, the fish in tow,
     and barked upon the shore.
A fire was there with fish and bread,
     that wasn't there before. (140)

"Bring of the fish you just now caught,"
        Son said to all of them,
But Peter climbed aboard the boat
        and pulled the net ashore.
A net un-torn, yet over-filled,
        for Peter's life, a sign,
For soon he will inform the world
        of Love's Song's theme sublime. (141)

He told them from this mission's start,
        that they would fish for men,
And thus He gave them Voice command
        to follow sacred call.
They would soon learn to follow Him,
        to fish with Love's Song's score,
To fill the net from many lakes,
        and pull the catch ashore. (142)

Son beckoned Peter afterward
        apart from all the rest,
"Do you, Simon, truly love Me,
        much more than you love these?"
"You know I do, Lord," Peter said,
        "You know I'll be Your friend."
To be a friend is not the same
        as love breathed by the Wind. (143)

For friendship's built on needs best met,
      and sometimes falls aside.
While love's indifferent to the needs,
      love loves because there's life.
As Love's love is for all the world
      and sent His only Son,
For rich and poor, for good and bad,
      regardless what's been done. (144)

So once again, "Do you love me?"
      the Son would query him.
"You know I do, Lord," Peter said,
      "You know I'll be Your friend."
Once again is the challenge made,
      and once again its feared,
A pride so hurt cannot forgive,
      the shame is too severe. (145)

"O.K. Simon, the son of John,
      will you then be my friend?"
It shot into his heart like fire
      and scorched its desert sand.
"You know all things. You are the Lord.
      You know I'll be Your friend."
So there it came from self contempt,
      at least there's no pretend. (146)

"When you were young, this pride gave you
       strong will to do all things,
But when you're old, you will be bound,
       led where you would not go."
Son sang Love's Song to such a one
       whose pride would not let go,
For he will love with love that's true,
       and die true love to show. (147)

"Feed My lambs, take care of My sheep,
       and feed My sheep," Son said.
Then, "Follow Me," sad Simon heard,
       the love was thus conveyed.
Forgiveness comes in many words,
       for love keeps no record,
Love is patient, and love is kind,
       and Peter is restored. (148)

For forty days the risen One
       met with the chosen ones,
And sang to them Love's Song replete
       and opened up their minds.
Assuring them He'd be with them
       throughout the coming age,
That they'd receive the Holy Wind,
       the ends of earth their stage. (149)

Then, soon one day near Bethany,
     before their very eyes,
The Son ascended in the clouds
     that hid Him from their sight.
The two in white were there again,
     "Why look into the sky?
He will come back as He has gone,
     on that you can rely." (150)

LOVE'S SONG TO THE BRIDE

CANTO OF WIND AND FIRE

Love's Song's best heard in desert hearts,
    where nothing's left to claim,
Where wisdom, knowledge of the self
    no longer chairs the pride.
When Son ascended to His throne,
    He promised such a space,
A Gift that Love had promise made,
    to give them Love's Song's Grace. (1)

But, His disciples must go back
    and wait for Love's great Gift,
And so they huddled in the place
    where they had first seen Him
As resurrected Son of God,
    where He had breathed on them,
Confirming them to send them forth
    to sing redemption's hymn. (2)

So there they spent this desert time
     in prayer for what will be,
That Son would fill the emptiness
     with Love's sweet promise made.
Some faithful women prayed there, too,
     and those who loved the Lord,
And Mary, mother of God's Son,
     all there in one accord. (3)

On Pentecost, the harvest feast
     which Hebrews celebrate
By thanking God for the first-fruits,
     the gathering of grain.
The ancient sign that Love had sung,
     a shadow of what's next,
The gathering of first in faith,
     the harvest of Elect. (4)

Now Love's Song is a desert song,
     where emptiness is made
By Wind that blows upon the heart,
     destroying what it claims,
By fire that purges all that's there,
     abolishing the dross,
Thus sifting mind and stripping pride,
     till all seems none but loss. (5)

When all of self is so denied,
    and willing to receive
The Way of truth and life made known,
    for truth will set one free.
And on this day of promise made,
    His own will hear the Wind,
And see the Fire that burns away
    the remnants to defend. (6)

For suddenly within that room,
    a violent Wind was heard,
Accompanied by tongues of Fire
    that sat on each of them.
They each were filled with Breath of God,
    the Fire of Holiness,
And spoke the Word that could be heard
    in tones of blessedness. (7)

As in that time before the time,
    creation was the aim,
Love knew full well what They would do,
    the order and the means.
That Word would say, then the display,
    what's not, became finite.
The Wind would sweep upon what's done
    and order it aright. (8)

So 'tis again that what They tend
      was new and made unique,
The Body giv'n; the Blood is shed;
      the new Way Word had made.
Love sacrificed and raised the Life
      that all might enter in.
Now Breath is given to the Song,
      that Truth be sung again. (9)

As many of the chosen race
      had stayed from Passover
To worship at the harvest feast
      just fifty days from then.
So there they were in temple courts,
      to celebrate the rite,
From every nation known to man
      were gathered at that site. (10)

Amazed, perplexed, they asked about,
      "What does this singing mean?
That we hear in our native tongue,
      the wonders of the Lord?"
But others mocked and wagged their heads,
      "These have had too much wine!"
Pride blindly spurts to shun in fear
      what it cannot define. (11)

Then Peter stood amidst them all
     and raised his voice aloud,
This Peter who before had feared
     was now with pow'r endowed,
"My fellow countrymen, give ear,
     let me explain the pow'r,
These are not drunk as you suppose;
     it's merely the third hour." (12)

'Tis this same Peter who denied
     and could not say he loved,
For he could not forgive himself
     to open up his heart.
But, when that day he was so filled
     with Breath of God above,
The Song was heard; he opened up,
     received the Gift of Love. (13)

"For this is That, the That of God,
     which Joel prophesied
To breathe afresh the Breath of Life,
     upon those who will hear,
With signs and wonders in the earth,
     and in the skies above,
When LORD would come in human flesh,
     to consummate the love." (14)

He then continued, filled with Breath,
    and singing from the heart.
He sang of Joel's prophecy
    of Spirit poured on all,
Of visions given to the young,
    and old men dreaming dreams,
Of men and women prophets filled
    and singing Love's Song's theme. (15)

He marked the age the last of days
    before the end of time,
Before the coming of the Lord,
    that great and awesome Day.
And sang Love's Song to desert hearts,
    hearts that were sin engraved,
That all who call upon the Name,
    would verily be saved. (16)

He sang of Son who came to them
    with wonders and with signs,
But how they had rejected Him
    and nailed Him to the cross.
He sang how Love had raised Him up,
    that death could not contain,
How all of this was planned by Love,
    that it was foreordained. (17)

In David's tomb there was the proof,
     where his remains were kept,
For he had sung of risen Lord
     unshaken on the throne,
Of hope he had of true life giv'n,
     and joy beyond the grave,
Of paths of life made known to all,
     of joy in God's conclave. (18)

That it was not a psalm that's sung
     of David on the throne,
But, of Another promised him,
     a kingdom yet to come,
Where King ascends to the right hand
     in Love's eternity,
To conquer pride, Love's enemy,
     redeeming destiny. (19)

And David's tomb was there to prove
     that he was not the One.
The Lord that David sang about
     was Peter's Song of Love.
"Therefore let all of Is'rel know,"
     he sang of sacrifice,
"That Love has raised the Crucified,
     for He is Lord and Christ." (20)

Love's Song's heard by deserted hearts,
     with Word that cuts the soul,
With Wind that blows the sands of pride,
     and Fire that burns what's dry.
"What shall we do?" the people wailed,
     for they had cursed I AM.
They knew full well that those who do
     were now among the damned. (21)

They crucified the very One
     that God had sent to save.
Now their very lives should be
     what Wind and Fire destroy.
But Love cannot forbid its own,
     specially if they see
That it's true love that pride has spurned
     and only love sets free. (22)

'Twas Love that hung upon the cross,
     and Love that put Him there,
"Forgive them, Father, for this wrong,
     they know not what they do."
They had not heard the Holy One,
     say 'mid the infamy,
Forgive them for rejecting Him,
     that He had set them free. (23)

Thus, Peter sang Love's perfect key
      that opened kingdom's door,
"Repent and be baptized each one,
      in the Messiah's Name,
And you will know forgiveness true,
      instead of wrath for sin.
With Breath of God you'll be endued,
      beginning life again." (24)

For Love had vowed in Adam's fall,
      to crush the head of pride,
Redeeming what was lost by man,
      when Love had been defied.
And Love had kept the promise live
      through Noah in the ark,
Freeing the chosen from the yoke,
      that blood on wood would mark. (25)

Love's Song was sung through ages past,
      that told of One to come,
Who'd be the Holy One of Love,
      the Seed of David's fame.
The Seed was God's; the womb was clean
      of Adam's dreadful deign.
He's now made known, this Son of God,
      within new hearts aflame. (26)

O mystery, O Love Divine,
      unseen in ages past,
But now disclosed to everyone,
      the riches of such love,
To call men out of pride's torment
      and set forever free,
'Tis Christ within the hearts of men,
      the hope of God's glory. (27)

Responding to Love's Song that day
      were some three thousand souls
Who did repent and were baptized
      to die to unbelief,
Who did confess the Holy Name
      they had blasphemed before,
Convinced by Word and Wind and Fire,
      and Love's Song's repertoire. (28)

Young Mary was the sign of this,
      when she in faith did ask,
"How will this be?" that Word's made flesh
      in such a one as me?
"Holy Spirit will come upon
      ...the pow'r of God will place."
And thus it was that Voice became
      a part of Adam's race. (29)

For Son's now born in each of us
      in this same manner shown
By she who in her virgin womb
      conceived the desert song.
And now the sign is thus fulfilled,
      but not by her alone,
But, by all who with open hearts,
      accept the Seed that's sown. (30)

THE CANTO OF THE BRIDE

The Son of Love now had a bride,
    who He in love called out,
Sung in the sacrifice of Love
    that seals the covenant,
That those who so elect the Way
    to live in Love's embrace,
Will truly one in body be
    with Son to birth Love's race. (1)

For Love's Song is a desert song,   2
    and fills the virgin mind
That makes the mother of the Son
    the Song's enduring sign.
As she was chosen full of grace,
    immaculate of heart,
So, too, the Bride by Son's own song
    is sealed and set apart. (2)

And as the Virgin shunned her pride
     and did not second guess,
As handmaid opened up herself
     to Word to work its grace,
So, too, the Bride accepts the Seed
     by which such grace imbues
The power to conceive and grow,
     and live a life that's new. (3)

So Mary is Bride's mother, too,
     for by her paradigm,
She brought to flesh the Word of Love,
     as all who hear the Song.
For generations to the end
     still call her "blessed" yet,
Whose Holy Child is still the Word
     by which new birth is set. (4)

And its His Way that woos the Bride,
     so she can ponder Him
Within her heart as Mary did,
     and Mystery impart.
And she it was who knew the Truth,
     though difficult to tell,
Thus, in such faith she showed the Way,
     thus letting it compel. (5)

As Mary took His body down,
      and held it in her hands,
So with His body and His blood
      the Bride the ages spans.
There she was in the upper room
      when Wind and Fire came down,
The Bride's assembled with the saints,
      receiving Love's Song's sound. (6)

Son loves the Bride and gives Himself
      in joy to meet her needs,
To make her holy, cleansing her
      with Water through the Word.
With His desire He has made known,
      presenting to His sight,
A blameless Bride, one blemish free,
      all radiant and bright. (7)

So Bride is sent into the world
      contending with the pride
That blights the image of the One
      who gave His Life to gain
A holy race to sing the Song
      that celebrates the Son,
To suffer what this love must bear
      to birth those who are won. (8)

The Bride and Groom are now made one
        in holy unity.
She is His Body, He her Head,
        and as she moves through time,
She sings in faith His Life and Truth
        in eremitic space,
And by His Word and Sacrament,
        to dance in His embrace. (9)

When the family she has borne
        as children of the King
Commune with Him at table set
        by His own sacrifice,
In eucharistic joy she sups,
        and then goes forth in deed,
Strengthened by this Bread and Cup,
        assisting those in need. (10)

She follows Him into the field,
        as Ruth so long ago,
To glean the harvest of the world,
        by bringing in the sheaves.
Thus, she is clothed in praise and joy,
        instead of sad despite,
And washed in water by the Word,
        anointed with delight. (11)

Disdaining pride and self conceit,
     she speaks with wisdom giv'n.
Its by the Wind she sings Love's Song
     and serves the least with grace.
By gifts bestowed by Love Themselves,
     she shows the greatest Way.
With patience, kindness, self-control,
     her love is on display. (12)

As Is'rel was the sign of her
     in wilderness of sin,
So Bride doth make her journey now,
     to reach the promised land.
With Manna from above she's fed,
     with Water from the Rock
She makes her way to Jordan's banks,
     eternal Love en-locked. (13)

LOVE'S ETERNAL SONG

CANTO OF THE WEDDING FEAST

Not all accept the Song of Love,
        not all will dance the Dance,
And time and space and history
        will wax into decay,
For pride will overtake the world
        through science and self-love,
Reject the Truth in ridicule,
        mock Wisdom from above. (1)

Salvation, power, kingdom reign,
        the power of the Son,
Have come through sacrifice of Love
        to overcome the pride.
The one who tempted Adam's race,
        has been thrown down by Him,
The Lamb of Love has shed the Blood
        that sings redemption's hymn. (2)

Thus they who hear and overcome,
     give testimony true,
Whose pride of life is dashed by grace,
     they're not afraid of death.
The devil is with fury filled,
     for he has lost the tort,
But still accuses day and night;
     he knows his time is short. (3)

Untruth and envy, evil works,
     ambition and deceit,
Aborting life for pleasure's sake,
     enamored with occult,
False gods will oft be glorified,
     and demons given place,
The Bride considered obsolete,
     Love's Song delusion's case. (4)

The Bride will stagger in the Dance,
     the Son be used as curse;
The tares among the wheat increase,
     ignorant of the Song,
And disbelief will replace faith,
     Indiff'rent to what's sung.
Dissent becomes the common tune,
     with leaven on the tongue. (5)

In just such times signs will appear
  that mark creation's song.
Creation's longed for such as this,
  with pains of birth she groans,
Forced in frustration's sordid grip,
  subjected to abuse,
With sin did come the clash with truth
  that caused decayed misuse. (6)

Creation has been in travail
  until this ordained time.
Creation, too, will be set free,
  when Son comes for His Bride.
Famines and earthquakes will make known
  the birth pangs that precede
The coming of the Son of Love,
  Beloved to receive. (7)

For Love's Song is a desert song
  and pride a desert makes,
That in the wasteland of the soul,
  there might be those who thirst
For precious water from the Rock,
  so stricken out of Love,
For the true manna, Bread of God,
  that's given from above. (8)

As in the ancient custom's rite,
    the groom comes for the bride.
With entourage of angel band,
    with trumpet and command,
So will the Son of Love descend
    to take His holy Spouse
To celebrate the wedding feast
    and enter Father's house. (9)

Those with true Oil in their own lamps,
    whose light is Spirit giv'n,
Who keep their watch while living on
    the cutting edge of time,
Will sing with such resplendent joy
    and join celestial choir,
Shout with the trumpets angels blow,
    rejoicing in this hour. (10)

Sing Hallelujah! Shout the sound,
    Lord God Almighty reigns,
Rejoice, be glad, the glory give,
    for Love Song's final verse:
The wedding of the Lamb has come,
    and ready is the Bride.
Her dress is white and bright and clean,
    there's nothing she would hide. (11)

He comes to reap on pure white steed;
    He's called Faithful and True;
He's King of kings and Lord of lords;
    His robe is dipped in Blood.
On His head are many crowns
    and from His mouth a sword
To strike the nations with His voice
    that wields eternal Word. (12)

From the four corners of the earth
    He gathers up His Bride,
First those who've gone through death's release,
    then after them the rest.
Earth and sky will forsake their place,
    rolled up as if a scroll,
And put to fire with space and time,
    pride's means of sin's control. (13)

And Lucifer still tries to hide,
    with those he has deceived,
With those whom he has tricked with pride,
    but un-truth desert made.
This radiant fire burns the chaff,
    is made an abyss lost,
And pride, his band, and all his kind
    are in it timeless tossed. (14)

For fire cannot redeem the blight
       that willful sin doth make.
No holocaust or sacrifice
       can cleanse the heart of stain,
But only Blood can cleanse the heart,
       and make for life anew,
'Tis only given by the Lamb,
       the only Blood that's true. (15)

Then the cosmos will pass away,
       and in its place revealed,
There is the Holy City bright;
       the Bride dressed for the Son.
And now the dwelling of the Love
       will be with all who've sung
This Love's Song in the desert place,
       all whom the Son has won. (16)

Time has fled and history read,
       so there's no moon nor sun.
There is no pride, so there's no shame,
       no shadow of deceit.
The glory of the Trinity
       is splendor's Light to see.
The Lamb its lamp for all to walk
       the Way eternally. (17)

The water's there, but from the Throne,
    it flows in purity,
And on each side the tree of life,
    with healing in its leaves.
The throne of Love and of the Lamb
    is this Bride's destiny,
And she will reign with Them in love,
    throughout eternity. (18)

The Love Song was a desert song,
    but now the desert's gone,
And so's the need to sing the Song;
    the love has been received.
The Bride's been sought, the dowry bought,
    for by His blood He won
The right to have Beloved stand
    beside Him at His throne. (19)

All that remains, a wedding feast,
    a banquet of great joy!
The Bride will sup in splendor there,
    with the bright Morning Star,
And drink Life's Water from the throne,
    for God is who it's from.
The Spirit and the Bride say "Come,"
    and those who hear say "Come." (20)

EPILOGUE

And so it is that Love's great plan,
    the enterprise of man,
Was in eternal thought of Them
    before creation's made.
That Love would have a Bride to sing
    in high celestial lays,
Of power, riches, wisdom, strength,
    and honor, glory, praise.

The seraphim, the cherubim,
    the myriads of hosts,
Were not the ones to fill the thought,
    could not a lover be.
The image and the likeness is
    for whom creation's made,
And only those whose am-ness flows
    with truth and spirit braid.

To reign with Them throughout non-time
    the goal was all along,
But love disrupted by the pride,
    would need to be redeemed.
There never was an absence of
    to reconcile the wrong,
And bring to bear upon sin's lair,
    the passion of Love's Song.

As blood did flow in garments made
      to cover nakedness,
So Blood would flow from God's own Lamb
      to bleach the stain of sin,
And gain for Son, once and for all,
      a holy, blameless Bride
To share the kingdom evermore,
      forever at His side.

The journey to ethereal plane
      oft led the prideful loved
Through desert times and desert place
      in order to redeem.
But at the proper time for Love,
      He sent His only Son
To show the love that melts the pride,
      and makes the besought one.

And that, beloved, is Love's Song
      that's sung for all to see
That Love's intent and will and gain
      throughout eternity
Is all along to have a Bride
      to share beyond decree.
What next will come that They might do
      in glory yet to be?

SCRIPTURE REFERENCES

LOVE'S SONG

CANTO OF LOVE'S SONG

1 - Genesis 1:1
2, 3 - Genesis 1:2
4 - Genesis 1:3, 6, 9, 11, 14, 20, 24
5 - Genesis 1:5, 8, 13, 19, 23, 31,   Gen. 2:1-3
6 - Genesis 1:3-19
7 - Genesis 1:20-25
8 - Genesis 1:31
9 - Genesis 1:26
10, 11, 12 - Genesis 1:26-30
13 - Genesis 2:16-17
14 - Genesis 2:7
15 - Genesis 1:27; Gen. 2:18, 20b-24
16 - Genesis 2:8-17
17 - Genesis 2:24-25
18 - Genesis 2:8-25

CANTO OF LOVE REJECTED

1 - Genesis 2:25
2, 3 - Isaiah 14:12-15
4 - Isaiah 14:15,; Luke 10:18
5, 6 - Genesis 3:1a
7, 8, 9 - Genesis 3:1b-4

(CANTO OF LOVE REJECTED)
10 - Genesis 3:5
11, 12 - Genesis 3:6; I John 2:16
13, 14 - Genesis 3:6b; Romans 12
15 - Genesis 3:7

CANTO OF LOVE'S FIDELITY

1, 2, 3 - Genesis 3:8-10
4, 5 - Genesis 3:11-13
6 - Genesis 3:14-15
7, 8, 9 - Genesis 3:16-20
10 - Genesis 3:21-24
11, 12 - Genesis 6:1-7
13 - Genesis 6:7-22
14 - Genesis 7:1-12
15 - Genesis 7:13-22

THE DESERT SONG

CANTO OF ABRAHAM

1, 2 - Genesis 12:1-3
3 - Genesis 12:4-8, 13:1-13
4 - Genesis 13:14-17
5, 6 - Genesis 16:1-2
7, 8 - Genesis 17:1-22
9 - Genesis 16:4-12
10, 11, 12 - Genesis 22:1-5

(CANTO OF ABRAHAM, CON'T)
13, 14, 15 - Genesis 22:6-12
16 - Genesis 22:12-14
17 - Genesis 22:15-18
18 - Romans 4:16-25; Heb. 11:17-19
19 - Genesis 32:22-30; 35:22b-28
20 - Genesis 37:12-35; 29:1-46:5
21 - Exodus 1:6-14

CANTO OF MOSES

1 - Exodus 1:15-22
2, 3 - Exodus 2:1-10
4, 5, 6 - Exodus 2:11-22
7 - Exodus 2:22b
8 - Exodus 2:23-25
9 - Exodus 3:1-3
10, 11, 12 - Exodus 3:4-13
13, 14, 15 - Exodus 3:14-4:1
16, 17, 18 - Exodus 4:2-17
19, 20, 21 - Exodus 4:18-31
22 - Exodus 5:1-21
23, 24 - Exodus 7:14-10:29
25 - Exodus 11:1-9
26, 27 - Exodus 12:1-20

CANTO OF SOJOURN

1 - Exodus 12:29-39
2 - Exodus 13:17-22
3 - Exodus 14:5-12
4, 5, 6 - Exodus 14:13-28
7 - Exodus 14:29-31
8, 9 - Exodus 15:22-27, 16:1-36
10, 11 - Exodus 17:1-7
12 - 1 Corinthians 10:1-4
13 - Exodus 19:1-13
14, 15 - Exodus 19:14-16; 20:1-31:18
16 - Numbers 13:1-29
17 - Numbers 14:1-4; 1 John 4:18
18 - Numbers 13:30-33; 14:15-10a, 10b-45
19, 20, 21 - Numbers 15:1-19:22
22, 23, 24 - Numbers 20:1-13
25, 26 - Numbers 20:12-13; Deuteronomy 32:49-52

CANTO OF DAVID

1 - Joshua 3:1-17
2 - Joshua 6 - 12; 13:8-21:45
3 - Judges 1:27-2:3; Judges 3:3ff
4 - 1 Samuel 1:1-2:11
5, 6 - 1 Samuel 3:1-3
7, 8, 9 - 1 Samuel 3:4-14
10 - 1 Samuel 3:15-4:1a
11, 12 - 1 Samuel 8:1-22
13 - 1 Samuel 9:1-2, 17; 10:1; 13:1

(CANTO OF DAVID, CON'T.)

14 - I Samuel 15:1-23
15 - I Samuel 16:1-13
16, 17 - I Samuel 16:14-23
18 - I Samuel 17:1-11
19, 20, 21 - I Samuel 17:26-51
22, 23 - I Samuel 18:5-16
24 - I Samuel 19:9-10
25 - I Samuel 22:1-2; 23:15-18; 24:1-22; 26:1-25
26 - I Samuel 30:21-25
27 - I Samuel 31:1-13

28 - II Samuel 1:18-27
29 - II Samuel 2:4
30 - II Samuel 5:1-5
31 - II Samuel 7:8-11a
32 , 33 - II Samuel 11:1-6
34, 35, 36 - II Samuel 11:7-27
37 - II Samuel 12:1-23
38 - II Samuel 13-18
39 - Psalm 51

CANTO OF THE PROPHETS

1 - I Kings 11:1-13
2, 3 - I Kings 13:1-34
4, 5, 6 - I Kings 11:26-39; 14:1-16
7, 8 - I Kings 16:29-33; 17:1-6
9 - I Kings 18:16-21
10, 11, 12 - I Kings 18:22-39

(CANTO OF THE PROPHETS, CON'T.)

13 - I Kings 18:40-46, 19:1-2
14, 15 - I Kings 19:3-9a
16, 17, 18 - I Kings 19:9b-13:a
19 - I Kings 19:3b-18
20,21 - II Kings 2:1-12
22 - II Kings 1:8; Matthew 3:4; Jude 9
23, 24 - II Kings 2:9-14
25 - II Kings 2:13-14
26, 27 - II Kings 2:19-8:15
28, 29, 30 - I Kings 22:8-28
31, 32, 33 - I Kings 22:8-28
34, 35, 36 - I Kings 22:8-28
37 - I Kings 22:28
38, 39 - I Kings 22:34-36
40 - Amos 1-9
41 - Hosea 1:1-2; 4:1-3
42 - Hosea 2:5-13; 8:7
43 - II Kings 17:7-23
44 - Hosea 14:9
45 - Isaiah 1:1; 2:12-21
46 - Isaiah 1:2-6
47, 48 - Isaiah 6:1-13
49 - Isaiah 6:8
50, 51 - Isaiah 24:4-13
52 - Isaiah 64:6-7
53 - Isaiah 35:1-2; 10:20-23; 35:3-7
54 - Isaiah 35:8-10

(CANTO OF THE PROPHETS, CON'T)

55 - Isaiah 7:14
56, 57 - Isaiah 9:6-7; 10:18-19; 11:1-9
58 - Isaiah 61:1-3
59 - Isaiah 53:1-12
60 - Isaiah 55: 1-13; 66:12-16
61 - Micah 1:1; 3:12
62 - Micah 4:1-2
63 - Micah 4:6-8; 6:3-5
64 - Micah 3:1-7
65 - Micah 5:2-5
66 - Zephaniah 1:2-5; Nahum 1:2-10; Habakkuk 2:4-16
67 - Zephaniah 1:14-2:3
68 - Nahum 3:1-4
69 - Habakkuk 1:2-4; 3:17-19
70 - Zephaniah 3:9-20
71 - Jeremiah 1:4-10; 13-15
72 - Jeremiah 31:29; 6:13-15
73 - Jeremiah 5:30-31
74 - Jeremiah 2:13
75 - Jeremiah 6:26-30; 8:21-22
76 - Jeremiah 26:7-11
77, 78 - Jeremiah 27:12-15; 52:12-16
79 - Ezekiel 1:1-2
80 - Ezekiel 1:4-14
81 - Ezekiel 1:15-28
82 - Ezekiel 2:1-8
83 - Ezekiel 4:1-5:17

THE DESERT DANCE

CANTO OF THE SON OF GOD

(CANTO OF THE SON OF GOD, CON'T.)
13, 14, 15 - Luke 1:26-33
16, 17 - Luke 1:34-38
18 - Galatians 4:4
19 - Isaiah 7:14
20, 21 - Luke 1:39-4
22 - John 1:14
23, 24 - Luke 1:46-53
25 - Luke 1:53-56
26, 27 - Matthew 1:18-25
28, 29, 30 - Luke 2:1-7
31, 32, 33 - Luke 2:7b
34, 35, 36 - Luke 2:8-16
37, 38 - Luke 2:17-20
39 - Luke 2:21-24
40, 41 - Luke 2:25-35
42 - Matthew 2:1-2
43 - Genesis 14:18-20; Hebrews 7:1, 14-17
44 - Matthew 2b
45 - Matthew 2:7-8; Isaiah 7:10-44
46 - Micah 5:2; Matthew 2:5-6
47, 48 - Matthew 2:7-10
49, 50, 51 - Matthew 2:11
52 - Matthew 2:12, 16-18
53, 54 - Jeremiah 31:15; Matthew 2:13
55 - Matthew 2:14-15; Hosea 11:1
56 - Matthew 2:21-24
57 - Luke 2:39-40

(CANTO OF THE SON OF GOD, CON'T.)

58 , 59, 60 - Luke 2:41-45

61 - Luke 2:46-50

62 - Luke 2:51-52

63 - Matthew 3:13

64 - Luke 1:76-79; 3:1-6

65, 66 - Luke 3:7-14

67, 68 - Matthew 3:1-5

69 - Matthew 3:6, 2 Kings 5:1-14; Genesis 1:1-5;
    I Peter 3:20-21a

70 - I Corinthians 10:2-4; Exodus 40:12-15; Revelation 1:15

71 - Acts 22:16; Hebrews 10:19-20; Romans 6:4

72 - Luke 3:16; Mark 1:7

73 - Matthew 3:11-12

74 - Matthew 3:13-15

75 - Romans 5:18-21; Hebrews 4:15; Philippians 2:6

76 - Hebrews 8:3-6; 9:11-15, 26b-28; 10:5-10

77 - II Samuel 7:16

78 - Psalm 110:1-4; Hebrews 6:20b-7:3

79 - Matthew 3:16-17

80 - Luke 4:1-2

81 - Luke 4:3, Genesis 3:6a

82 - Matthew 4:4; Luke 4:4; Deuteronomy 8:3

83, 84 - Luke 4:5-8; Genesis 3:6b; Deuteronomy 6:13

85, 86, 87 - Luke 4:9-11; Psalm 91:11-12

88 - Luke 4:12; Genesis 3:6c

89 - Luke 4:13; Deuteronomy 6:16; I John 2:16-17

90 - John 1:5; Ephesians 6:10-18

91 - Luke 4:13b

CANTO OF THE SONG OF LOVE

1 - Hebrews 4:12
2 - John 8:58
3 - Luke 4:14-17
4, 5 - Luke 4:18-21
6 - Luke 4:22-24
7 - Luke 5:1-11, 27-32
8 - Matthew 5:3-7:29
9 - Matthew 8:3-10:42
10 - John 2:1-25; Luke 8:26-56; John 9:1-41
11 - Matthew 8:1-9:8; 14:13-33; Luke 8:10-17; John 9:1-41
12 - Luke 9:46-10:42; Luke 18:18-19:10
13 - Matthew 5:17-32
14 - Matthew 5:453-48; 18:15-35; 22:34-49
15 - John 13:34; 15:9-47; 13:1-17
16, 17 - Matthew 13:1-52
18 - Matthew 17:1-13
19 - Psalm 85:10-11; Romans 14:13-18;
    Colossians 1:26-28

CANTO OF THE DANCE

1 - Luke 2:25-35; John 11:45-57
2 - Matthew 23:16 (1-39)
3 - John 14:6; 8:58
4 - Isaiah 14:12-15; John 8:44; Luke 10:18; 20:19
5 - Ephesians 1:3-10

(CANTO OF THE DANCE, CON'T.)

6 - Exodus 12:1-20

7 - Matthew 21:1-11; John 12:12-16 (Revelation 7:9-10)

8 - Matthew 21:14-16

9 - Matthew 18:1-4; 19:13-15

10 - John 12:20-33

11 - Matthew 26:17-19 (Exodus 12:14-20)

12 - John 13:1-5

13, 14, 15 - John 13:6-21

16 - Matthew 26:20-25

17 - Matthew 26:26; Luke 22:14-19

18 - Matthew 26:27-28; Luke 22:20

19, 20 - John 6:53-60, 67-70

21 - Matthew 26:27-30

22 - Matthew 26:1-5; John 13:26-30

23 - Luke 22:21-30; Romans 11:33-36

24 - Matthew 26:31-35

25, 26 - Matthew 26:31-35

27 - Matthew 26:36-39; John 17

28 - Matthew 26:40-44

29 - John 12:27-33; Luke 22:41-44

30 (Isaiah 53:10) Mark 14:41-42

31 - John 3:16-21

32 - John 18:1-3

33 - Luke 22:47-55; John 3:20

34, 35, 36 - John 18:4-7

37 - John 18:6-8

38 - Matthew 26:50b-51

(CANTO OF THE DANCE, CON'T.)

39 - Matthew 26:52-68

40, 41, 42 - Luke 22:54c-62

43 - Matthew 26:59-66

44, 45 - Matthew 27:3-5a

46 - Matthew 27:5b; Mark 14:61b-66; John 18:28

47, 48 - Luke 23:2-11

49, 50, 51 - Luke 23:13-23

52 - Matthew 27:24-26

53 - John 19:1-3; Isaiah 53:5b

54 - Matthew 27:27-31

55, 56, 57 - Luke 23:26-31

58, 59, 60 - Matthew 27:33-35, 39-40; John 19:23-24;
            Mark 15:27-32 (Isaiah 52:14; 53:3)

61 - Matthew 26:39

62 - Luke 23:33-34a

63 - Matthew 27:39-40; John 2:19-22; Luke 23:39

64, 65 - Luke 23:40-43

66 - John 19:25-27

67 - John 19:25-27

68, 69 - Luke 23:44-45a; Mark 15:33-34

70 - John 1:3-5

71 - John 1:29-34

72 - Hebrews 10:5-10; John 4:34; 6:38-40; 12:23-33

73 - Isaiah 53:7, 10

74 - Matthew 16:21-28; Hebrews 9:14

75 - John 19:28

76, 77 - John 19:29; Matthew 27:48

(CANTO OF THE DANCE, CON'T.)

78 - Luke 22:14-20; John 6:53-56

79 - John 19:30a

80 - Luke 23:46

81 - Matthew 27:51-53

82, 83, 84 - John 19:31-33; Luke 22:19; Philippians 2:8

85 - Exodus 12:43-46; 12:17-20; John 19:33-36

86 - Luke 22:19; John 15:12-13

87 - Romans 5:12-19, Ephesians 1:3-4

88 - John 19:34-37; I Corinthians 11:27-33

89 - I Peter 1:18-20; I Corinthians 11:23-27

90 - John 19:38-42

91 - Luke 2:34-35; Luke 1:34-35

92 - Matthew 12:38-40; John 2:18-22

93 - I Peter 3:18-20a; John 5:24-29; Luke 1:76-79

94 - I Corinthians 15:55-57

95 - Romans 6:3-10

96 - Hebrews 9:14

97 - Hebrews 10:9; Colossians 1:13-14

98 - Matthew 16:18; Revelation 1:18

99 - Ephesians 4:7-10

100 - Revelation 1:18; Acts 2:24-31

101, 102 - John 12:23-33; Romans 8:37-39

103 - Exodus 17; Revelation 21:6-7; Psalm 23:1-4;
   Revelation 7:17

104 - John 5:6-8

105 - Genesis 3:15; Revelation 12:10-12

106 - Matthew 28:2

(CANTO OF THE DANCE, CON'T.)

107, 108 - I Peter 1:10-12; Matthew 26:53-54

109 - Philippians 2:6-11; I Corinthians 15:17-28

110 - I Peter 1:3-5

111 - I Peter 1:8-9

112, 113 - Matthew 28:4; Luke 24:1-8

114 - Luke 24:9-12; John 20:3-6a

115, 116, 117 - John 20:6b-10

118, 119, 120 - John 20:10-17a; 17:24

121 - Ephesians 3:17b-19

122 - John 20:17b-18

123 - Luke 24:13-18

124, 125, 126 - Luke 24:19-27

127 - Luke 24:24-32

128 - Luke 22:14-20; John 6:53-58

129 - John 6:62-69

130, 131, 132 - John 20:19-25; I John 4:18

133, 134, 135 - John 20:26-29

136, 137, 138 - John 21:2-6

139, 140, 141 - John 21:7-11; Genesis 3:7-10

142 - Luke 5:1-11; Matthew 28:18-20

143 - John 21:15

144 - John 3:16-21

145, 146, 147 - John 21:16-18

148 - John 21:15-17, 19b; I Corinthians 13:4a

149 - Acts 1:3-5

150 - Luke 24:50; Acts 1:6-11

LOVE'S SONG TO THE BRIDE

CANTO OF WIND AND FIRE

1 - Matthew 5:3; I Corinthians 1:18-31; Luke 24:45-49
2 - Luke 24:47-49; Acts 1:12-13a
3 - Acts 1:13b-14
4 - Leviticus 23:15-21
5 - Luke 3:16-17
6 - Acts 2:1
7 - Acts 2:2-4
8 - Genesis 1:1-5
9 - Matthew 9:15-17; Hebrews 10:20-23; John 4:23-24
10, 11, 12 - Acts 2:5-15
13, 14, 15 - Acts 2:16-21
16, 17, 18 - Acts 2:22-31; Psalm 16:8-11
19, 20, 21 - Acts 2:32-31
22, 23 - Luke 23:34-35
24 - Acts 2:38
25 - Genesis 3:15; I Peter 3:18-21
26, 27 - Colossians 1:26-27
28 - Acts 2:41
29 - Luke 1:34-38
30 - John 1:14; I Peter 1:22-23; John 3:3-8

THE CANTO OF THE BRIDE

1 - Ephesians 5:25-32
2 - Luke 1:28-32; Song of Songs 7:9b-8:7
3 - 1 Peter 1:23; Revelation 12:1-17
4 - Song of Songs 4:8-15; Luke 1:45-50; 1 Peter 1:23
5 - Isaiah 61:10-11
6 - 1 Corinthians 10:16-17; Acts 1:14; John 19:25-27
7 - Ephesians 5:25-27
8 - Revelation 12:10-17
9 - Ephesians 5:30-32
10 - Isaiah 54:1-10; Acts 2:42-47
11 - Ruth 2:2-3, 7; Micah 4:12; Psalm 126:5-6
12 - Galatians 5:16-25; 1 Corinthians 12:7-11, 31-13:8a
13 - 1 Corinthians 10:1-6; John 6:31-40

LOVE'S ETERNAL SONG

CANTO OF THE WEDDING FEAST

1 - II Timothy 3:1-9; James 3:13-18; II Thessalonians 2:9-12
2, 3 - Revelation 12:10-12; 5:9-10
4 - II Peter 2:1-3, 10b-12
5 - Matthew 13:24-43; 16:5-12
6 - 1 Corinthians 5:6-8; Jude 8-19; Revelation 3:11-16
7 - Romans 8:18-22; Mark 13:5-8
8 - John 6:38-40; 7:37-39
9 - Matthew 22:1-14; 25:1-13; 1 Thessalonians 4:16-17;
  Revelation 19:11-16

(CANTO OF THE WEDDING FEAST, CON'T.)

10 - Matthew 25:1-13

11, 12 - Revelation 19:6-9, 11-16

13 - II Peter 3:10-14; Revelation 6:12-7:12

14, 15 - Revelation 20:1-15

16, 17, 18 - Revelation 21:9-22:5

19, 20 - Revelation 3:21; 5:9-10; 22:1-5, 14-17

Printed in the United States
221983BV00002B/5/P